Western Baptist Educational Convention

Proceedings of the Western Baptist Educational Convention

held in the First Baptist Church, Chicago, May 24 and 25, 1871

Western Baptist Educational Convention

Proceedings of the Western Baptist Educational Convention
held in the First Baptist Church, Chicago, May 24 and 25, 1871

ISBN/EAN: 9783337264154

Printed in Europe, USA, Canada, Australia, Japan

Cover: Foto ©Lupo / pixelio.de

More available books at **www.hansebooks.com**

PROCEEDINGS

OF THE

WESTERN BAPTIST

EDUCATIONAL CONVENTION,

HELD IN THE

FIRST BAPTIST CHURCH, CHICAGO,

MAY 24 AND 25, 1871.

PUBLISHED BY THE CONVENTION.

CHICAGO:
THE LAKESIDE PUBLISHING AND PRINTING COMPANY,
108 AND 110 DEARBORN STREET.
1871.

NOTE.

The reports of addresses made during the session of the Convention are for the most part copied from the columns of "The Standard."

PROCEEDINGS

OF THE

WESTERN BAPTIST

EDUCATIONAL CONVENTION.

FIRST DAY'S PROCEEDINGS.

MORNING SESSION.

The Western Baptist Educational Convention assembled in the First Baptist Church, Chicago, at nine o'clock, and was called to order by the Secretary of the American Baptist Educational Commission, Rev. S. S. Cutting, D.D.

The following is the list of Visitors and Delegates present:

ROLL OF VISITORS AND DELEGATES.

NEW HAMPSHIRE.

VISITORS.—Rev. W. H. Eaton, D.D.; Rev. C. II. Richardson.

VERMONT.

VISITORS.—Rev. Narcisse Cyr; Rev. C. F. Nicholson.

MASSACHUSETTS.

VISITORS.—Rev. B. F. Bronson, D.D.; Rev. S. W. Foljambe, D.D.; Rev. C. F. Foster; Rev. Alvah Hovey, D.D.; Rev. W. B. Thompson; Rev. James Upham, D.D.

RHODE ISLAND.

VISITOR.—Rev. S. L. Caldwell, D.D.

CONNECTICUT.

VISITORS.—Rev. Amasa Howard; Wm. J. Leonard; Rev. S. D. Phelps, D.D.; Rev. Robert Turnbull, D.D.

NEW YORK.

VISITORS.—Pres't M. B. Anderson, LL.D.; W. F. Benedict; J. C. Corning; H. M. Congar; J. Durfey; Cyrus W. Hatch; Rev. L. P. Judson; John A. Pearson; Rev. Wm. Rees; Smith Sheldon; James M. Sutherland; W. Sutherland; Charles Truax.

NEW JERSEY.

VISITORS.—Rev. W. H. Parmeley, D.D.; Hon. P. P. Runyan; Rev. D. H. Miller, D.D.; Rev. Joseph Banvard, D.D.

PENNSYLVANIA.

VISITORS.—H. G. Weston, D.D.; Rev. W. S. Goodno.

4 WESTERN BAPTIST

SOUTH CAROLINA.

VISITORS.—Rev. E. T. Winkler, D.D.; Hon. Wm. E. Wording, LL.D.

LOUISIANA.

VISITOR.—Rev. R. R. Whittier.

OHIO.

DELEGATES.

Denison University.—President Samson Talbot, D.D.; Rev. A. H. Strong D.D.; Rev. I. N. Carman; E. Thresher; Rev. N. A. Read.

Baptist Education Society.—Rev. D. A. Randall; Rev. D. Shepardson D.D.; Rev. Marsena Stone, D.D.; Prof. J. Stevens; J. H. Tangerman.

Mt. Auburn Young Ladies Seminary.—Rev. J. C. C. Clarke.

VISITORS.

Rev. F. L. Chappell; James L. Cox; Rev. F. A. Douglass; C. R. Dunbar Rev. J. Huntington; Rev. Reuben Jeffery, D.D.; Rev. C. D. Morris; Rev E. A. Taft.

MICHIGAN.

DELEGATES.

Kalamazoo College.—President Kendall Brooks, D.D.; Hon. Caleb Va Husen; Rev. Geo. W. Harris; Rev. H. L. Morehouse; Rev. A. E. Mathe

Kalamazoo Theological Seminary.—Rev. Samuel Graves, D.D.; Rev. J Donnelly, Jr.; Rev. James F. Hill; Rev. T. Z. R. Jones; Rev. Andrew Ten breck; Rev. T. M. Shanafelt.

Michigan Baptist Education Society.—H. C. Briggs; Rev. A. Owen; Rev E. J. Fish; Rev. L. C. Pattengill.

Fenton Seminary.—J. Cranston; Rev. L. Wadney.

VISITORS.

Rev. F. B. Cressey; Rev. James S. Cox; Rev. J. Mathews; Prof. Edwar Olney; H. B. Taft; Rev. O. D. Taylor.

INDIANA.

DELEGATES.

Franklin College.—President H. L. Wayland, D.D.; Rev. O. Ayer; Rev J. S. Boyden; Rev. Wm. Elgin; Rev. A. J. Essex; Rev. L. D. Robinson Rev J. R. Stone.

Crown Point Institute.—Rev. T. H. Ball.

VISITORS.

Rev. A. A. Carpenter; E. K. Chandler; A. B. Chapin; Rev. J. C. Fernald Rev. D. S. French; Rev. Geo E. Leonard; Rev. F. Mace; Rev. O. P. Meek Rev. J. J. W. Place; Rev. T. Reese; Rev. H. Smith; Rev. Silas Tucker, D.L

ILLINOIS.

DELEGATES.

Illinois Baptist Education Society.—Prof. Washington Leverett; H. N Kendall.

Shurtleff College.—Rev. J. Bulkley, D.D.; Rev. N. M. Wood, D.D.; Pro O. Howes.

University of Chicago.—Prof. J. W. Stearns; Rev. Charles Button.

Baptist Theological Seminary.—President G. W. Northrup, D.D.; A. N Arnold, D.D.; E. C. Mitchell, D.D.; R. E. Pattison, D.D.

Baptist Theological Union.—C. N. Holden; J. E. Tyler; W. W. Evert; D.D.; Edward Goodman; G. S. Bailey, D.D.

Almira College.—President J. B. White; Rev. J. Cole.

VISITORS.

Rev. W. W. Ames; Rev. E. N. Archibald; Rev. J. M. Gregory, LL.D. Rev. F. E. Arnold; Rev. J. Y. Aitchison; Rev. L. C. Bates; L. T. Bush James P. Cadman; Rev. J. Cairns; Charles Carlstadt; Rev. D. F. Carna han; Rev. C. W. Clark; Rev. T. C. Clendenning; Rev. J. D. Cole, D.D.

Rev. R. R. Coon; Rev. C. T. Emerson; Rev. Henry L. Field; Rev. M. L. Fuller; Rev. E. A. Gastman; Rev. William Green; Rev. W. M. Haigh; Rev. J. C. Hart; Rev. C. E. Hewitt; Rev. E. W. Hicks; Rev. E. L. Hunt; Rev. F. W. Ingmire; Rev. W. B. James; W. A. Jarrell; Rev. W. J. Kermott; Rev. H. Kingsbury; Wm. Lawrence; Rev. J. T. Mason; Rev. J. F. Merriam; C. H. Moffat; Rev. T. C. Morely; Rev. H. E. Norton; Rev. R. M. Nott; J. Pennoyer; Rev Geo Phippen; Rev. N. Pierce; Rev. Thos. Platt; Rev Thos. T. Potter; Rev. Thos. Powell; Rev. Volney Powell; E. F. Price; Rev. L. Raymond; Rev. J. A. Smith, D.D.; Rev. W. H. Stifler; Rev. Silas Thomas; Rev. M. M. Took; Rev. C. T. Tucker; Rev. A. N. Walter; Rev. H. B. Waterman; Rev J. T. Westover; Rev. J. M. Whitehead; W. A. Wilson; Rev. J. L. M. Young; Rev. Leroy Church.

MISSOURI.

DELEGATES.

William Jewell College.—Rev. A. H. Burlingham, D D.; Rev. D. T. Morrill; Rev. J W. Warder; Prof. Norman Fox.

VISITORS.

Rev. S. W. Marston; Rev. George Kline; Rev. Thomas Hudson.

IOWA.

DELEGATES.

Desmoines University.—Rev. J. V. Schofield; Rev. Luther Stone; Rev. J. W. Denison.

Iowa Baptist Union.—Rev. Thomas Brande; Rev. J. F. Childs; Rev. D. H. Cooley; Rev. S. K. Leavitt; Rev. Dexter P. Smith, D.D.

Cedar Valley Seminary.—Prof. Alvah Bush; Rev. H. H. Burrington; Rev. A. T. Cole; O. A. Goodhue, M.D.; Rev. Asa Marsh.

VISITORS.

Rev. George M. Adams; Rev. F. Adkins; Hon. J M. Beck; Rev. C. Brooks; F. M. Bruner; Rev. N. S. Burton, D.D.; Rev. R. A. Clapp; Rev. O. L. Crittenden; Prof. Amos N. Currier; Rev. R. R Hawley; Rev. L. W. Hayhurst; Rev. Robert Leslie; A. Mink; Rev. C. H. Remington; Rev. E. P. Savage; Rev. J. N. Seeley; Rev P. S. Whitman.

WISCONSIN.

DELEGATES.

Wayland University.- -Rev. O. O. Stearns; Rev. J. E. Johnson; A. Joy; Prof. J. A. Miner; Hon. C. Burchard.
Baptist Education Society.—Rev. J. W. Fish; Prof. A. S. Hutchins; Rev. E. Nesbit. D.D.

VISITORS.

B. L Aldrich; Rev. N. E. Chapin; Rev. Henry Clark; Rev. L. Fosdic; Prof. Milo P. Jewett. LL.D.; Dr. L. E. Ober; Rev. E. H. Page; E. C. Smith; G. D. Stevens; Rev. J. T. Sunderland; Rev. J. M. Titterington; Rev. J. H. Wilderman; N. E. Word; Rev. Isaac B. Branch, D.D.S.

MINNESOTA.

DELEGATES.

Baptist State Convention.—Rev. L. B. Allen, D D.; Hon. Mark H. Dunnell, LL.D.; Rev. A. Gale; Rev. E. B. Hurlburt; Rev. Daniel Read, LL.D.

VISITORS.

Rev. G. W. Fuller; D. D. Merrill; Rev. L B Teft.

NEBRASKA.

VISITOR.—Rev. J. W. Daniels.

CANADA.

VISITORS.—Rev. R. A. Fyfe, D.D; Rev. John Bates; Rev. H. W. Stearns.

The following Board of Permanent Officers was elected by the Convention:

EBENEZER THRESHER, of Ohio, *President.*
HON. J. M. GREGORY, LL.D.. of Illinois, ⎱ *Vice Presidents.*
HON. CALEB VAN HUSEN, of Michigan, ⎰
REV. E. C. MITCHELL, D D., of Illinois, *Secretary.*

Prayer was offered by the Rev. W. W. Everts, D.D., of Illinois.

The business of the Convention was then introduced with an address by Rev. Dr. Cutting, setting forth the objects of the Convention and suggesting an Order of Exercises as follows:

WEDNESDAY MORNING AND AFTERNOON.

1. The Question of Academies in the Scheme of Higher Education, including that of Preparatory Departments in our Colleges, and the bearing upon this question of the Existence of Public High Schools. Prof. J. W. Stearns, University of Chicago.

2. The Question of the Education of the Women of the West, including that of the Admission of both Sexes to the same Institutions of Higher Learning. Rev. H. L. Wayland, D.D., President of Franklin College, Ind.

3. The Place of Scientific Studies in Present Education. Rev. Samson Talbot, D.D., President of Denison University, Ohio.

WEDNESDAY EVENING.

4. The Colleges and Universities of the West, their Present Character and Functions, with the possible Lines of their Development, to meet the Advancing Needs of Education. Rev. J. A. Smith, D.D., Chicago.

THURSDAY MORNING AND AFTERNOON.

5. How Christian Institutions of Higher Learning, Academies, Colleges, Universities, and Theological Seminaries, keeping progress with the growth of Society, can best be built up in the West, with due regard always to other necessary expenditures of money for religious purposes. A Discussion, to be opened by Dr. Bulkley, of Shurtleff College.

6. The Duties of Western Churches with reference to the Perpetuation, Increase, and Education of the Ministry. Rev. Kendall Brooks, D.D., President Kalamazoo College, Mich.

7. The Care of Education as part of Pastoral Duty, with the bearing of a general and effective movement in education on the Character, Progress, and Usefulness of the Denomination. Rev. J. V. Schofield, DesMoines Iowa.

The Order of Exercises suggested by Dr. Cutting was adopted.

The following Committees were appointed:

Committee on Delegates:

Rev. J. F. CHILDS, of Iowa.
Rev. S. WASHINGTON, of Ill.
Rev. E. K. CHANDLER, of Ind.
Rev. SILAS THOMAS, of Ill.

Committee on Academies.

Rev. R. M. NOTT, of Ill.
Rev. A. OWEN, of Mich.
Rev. GEO. KLINE, of Mo.
Rev. D. H. COOLEY, of Iowa.
Prof. A. S. HUTCHINS, of Wis.
Rev. I. N. CARMAN, of Ohio.
Rev. L. B. ALLEN, D.D., of Minn.

Committee on Colleges and Universities.

Prof. A. N. ARNOLD, D.D., of Ill.
Rev. DANIEL READ, LL.D., of Minn.
Prof. ALVAH BUSH, of Iowa.
Prof. NORMAN FOX, of Mo.
Rev. A. J. ESSEX, of Ind.
Rev J. C. C. CLARKE, of Ohio.
Prof M. P. JEWETT, LL D., of Wis.

Committee on Scientific Education.

Prof. EDWARD OLNEY, of Mich.
Prof. A. N. CURRIER, of Iowa.
Prof. O. HOWES, of Ill.
Rev. J. E. JOHNSON, of Wis.

Committee on the Increase of the Ministry and Theological Education.

Rev. N. M. WOOD, D.D., of Ill.
Rev. A. H. BURLINGHAM, D.D., of Mo.
Rev. E. NESBIT, D.D., of Wis.
Rev. SILAS TUCKER, D.D., of Ind.
Rev. D. P. SMITH, D.D., of Iowa.
Rev. F. A. DOUGLASS, of Ohio.

Committee on Denominational Work in Education.

Rev. G. W. NORTHRUP, D.D., of Ill.
Rev. A A. KENDRICK, of Mo.
Prof. JOHN STEVENS, of Ohio.
Rev. O. O. STEARNS, of Wis.
Rev. SAMUEL GRAVES, D.D., of Mich.
Rev. S. L. CALDWELL, D.D., of R. I.
Rev. LEMUEL MOSS, DD., of Pa.

Committee on Education of Women.

Hon. MARK H. DUNNELL, LL.D., of Minn.
Rev. JOHN B. WHITE, of Ill.
Judge J. M. BECK, Iowa.
Rev. DANIEL SHEPARDSON, D.D., of Ohio.
Rev. D. T. Morrill, Mo.

The Convention then proceeded to listen to a paper, by Prof. J. W. Stearns, of the University of Chicago, upon

THE QUESTION OF ACADEMIES IN A SCHEME OF HIGHER EDUCATION, INCLUDING THAT OF PREPARATORY DE-PARTMENTS IN OUR COLLEGES, AND THE BEARING UPON THIS QUESTION OF THE EXISTENCE OF PUBLIC HIGH SCHOOLS.

I propose to discuss briefly: 1st, the reason of the neglect of Secondary Education at the West; 2dly, whether Preparatory Departments are adequate to furnish this education; 3dly, whether High Schools can be depended on to furnish it; and 4thly, what is necessary to constitute a good Academy

I. Three facts in our educational arrangements seem to me especially sig-nificant: that the public school system makes the primary school its point of departure; that the voluntary system tends to the production of colleges in excess of the wants of the community; and that secondary education is so far neglected as to be made either incidental — an unwelcome but necessary appendage to the college — or else quite inadequate; in short, that in attempting to seat it upon two stools, we have allowed it to fall to the ground between them   We must seek to understand what these facts mean.

I find the explanation of them in the different aims of the two educational systems. In this country, public schools are regarded as a governmental necessity. They have grown out of the conviction that the permanence and well-being of a republic depend upon the intelligence of the great body of her citizens. This conviction determines their aim, which is to leave as small a number of children as possible to grow up in dangerous ignorance. Therefore the primary school is of the first importance. Moreover, the character and tendency of the instruction which the schools afford is decided by the same consideration. Their ruling purpose is to train the young for the practical duties of citizenship and of business life. The public schools, in short, seek to meet the wants of the majority. The tendency with them, therefore, is to overestimate the present and the practical, and to disregard the past and the speculative.

The voluntary system is mostly under the direction of the Church. It, too, has a definite aim, but one materially different from the preceding. This is to develop leaders of men. Hence higher education is its province, and the college is its point of departure, the vital element of the system. The kind of instruction afforded is determined by the end sought. Two things are essential to good leadership — breadth of view, which can only be obtained by a knowledge of other times, other people, and other ways of thinking than those in the midst of which we live; and wisdom, which grows out of a knowledge of what men have tried, and what men have accom-plished in the past. These things are absolutely essential to the training of good leaders, able to think independently and to act prudently. Moreover, the Church wisely seeks to give that culture which will keep alive a sense of the great revolution wrought in human life by the introduction of Chris-tianity. Now, these three purposes tend to one and the same result, to give prominence, in this scheme of instruction, to what has been somewhat con-temptuously styled "antiquarianism." With such ends in view, it is mani-fest, again, that the voluntary system must make the college its point of departure. its head-centre of impulse and inspiration. Feeling this, each denomination of Christians, in inaugurating its educational work in a new State, seeks to lay, as soon as possible, the foundations of such an institu-tion. The tendency, thus arising, to exceed the actual wants of the commu-nity, is further encouraged by the confidence of rapid growth which is char-acteristic of a new country, and which requires provision to be made, not only for the present, but also for the certain future. Then comes the strug-gle for existence, which, if we are to believe certain scientific teachings, is not particularly favorable to the success of the weaker sort.

We can not hope to change this order of development. The fault in it, if there is any, is the assumption that State lines are natural boundaries in educational work, so that an entire system must be created in each State by each denomination. If this is a mistake, it can be remedied only, so far as I can see, by experience, and by causing the importance and necessity of sec-ondary education to be more generally recognized.

From this view of the principles which have determined the development of the two systems, we at once see why secondary education has been neg-lected. It lies between the college and the primary school. It is, therefore, incidental to both systems, and only incidental. Both do something to pro-mote it. The State scheme looks forward to it as in the line of its progress, and provides for it as well as can be done consistently with the prosecution of its main work. I hope to be able to show, however, that high schools can never be depended upon as the chief source of supply for our colleges. It is self evident that they can not at the present time. The voluntary system has therefore taken up the work, as indispensable to its higher institutions. The colleges have been compelled to provide academic teaching, and they have done so by the expedient of preparatory departments.

II. Is this expedient wise, and adequate to the necessity? I can not regard it as unwise, although it is certainly attended with some serious disadvantages. There are difficulties of management arising from the great disparity of age and attainments in the pupils; there is the sentimental objection — to which we may attach more or less importance, according to our point of view,— that a college suffers a certain loss of dignity by having such an attachment; there is a constant tendency to overload the instructors (by no means a sentimental objection), and, by reducing them to mere drudges, to prevent them from attaining the best results in their proper work. While the college is thus injured, the academy also is liable to suffer, from the fact that it is looked upon as an appendage, and its claims are likely to be treated as subsidiary to others. But the expedient has this one great recommendation, that in earlier stages of our educational work it has made it possible to have colleges at all. I might go further, and say that if we could disabuse ourselves of the idea that by the arrangement we are carrying on two separate institutions, and could organize a single course of instruction of eight or nine years, beginning with the secondary grade, I think such a plan would be attended with very considerable advantages.

The objection to preparatory departments as a means of providing for secondary education, does not lie chiefly in the direction already indicated. Even if we admit that they are, on the whole, a serious disadvantage to the institutions with which they are connected, we still have to acknowledge that at present our colleges can not live without them. To cut them off is like cutting off the right hand. I liken them rather to the cotyledons which the young plant pushes up with its growth, and feeds upon until it has attained sufficient strength to live without them. The only way in which we can hope to get rid of them is so to swell the college classes that they shall be felt to be merely incumbrances. Why is not this accomplished? Among other reasons, as it seems to me, because the expedient of preparatory departments is an utterly inadequate one to encourage and support such a growth.

Looking at the condition of the voluntary educational system in this State as fairly indicative of that prevailing generally in the West, I find that there are twenty-one colleges in Illinois, all but two of which have preparatory departments. Four years ago, every college in the State had such a department. Not only does the number of pupils in the preparatory departments far exceed that of those in attendance on the colleges, but the number of the latter is very small. Four years ago, fourteen of the best colleges in the State graduated, on an average, less than eleven pupils each, and only one as many as twenty. Many reasons might be assigned for this state of affairs, but the most important one, I think, is, that the colleges are little better than local institutions. Most of their pupils come from a comparatively limited field, in which the influence of the college is powerfully felt. So long as our colleges depend chiefly upon their own preparatory departments as feeders, this must necessarily be the case.

Preparatory departments, then, can not take the place of academies in fostering and developing a wide-spread interest in liberal culture. That kind of an influence which they exert in the communities where they are situated, ought to be developed in a great many different centres, all subsidiary to the one institution. We need academies, ably conducted and judiciously located, to exercise this influence. They would draw to themselves a great many young persons who, but for the neighborhood of such a school, would never think of obtaining an education. They would inspire a desire for higher culture in the minds of pupils who entered them with very limited expectations They would be operating powerfully in building up the higher institutions, not only by increasing the number of pupils in attendance upon them, but by drawing towards them the thoughts and affections of the people over a very large field of operations. We can not any longer sit still and wait for the colleges to grow. We can not make them exert the widest and most salutary influence, even by swelling their endowments and increasing their facilities for instruction, essential as this is. We must organize our system. We must put in operation the train of causes which draw men to these institutions. We must come into connection with the people as extensively as possible, and make them to feel, in every way in our power, the importance of the work we are trying to do. To talk of accomplishing this by preparatory departments, is as absurd as to maintain that large churches, built at the county-seats, would be better means of promoting the growth of religion than the small chapels are, which now spring up in every village.

But, in the second place, preparatory departments can not take the place of academies, because the latter ought to be something more than schools of preparation for college. They ought to be this above everything else, to be the quiet streams which drift everything on their surface towards the larger river; but they ought also to furnish supplementary instruction to that of the district schools. This they should do, because instruction of this kind is made accessible by our public school system to only a portion of the people. High schools can not exist except in the larger towns. They afford free instruction only to the children of those who are taxed to support them. Their courses of study, regulations and general arrangements, are always adapted to the wants of the city, and consequently are, in many respects, not well suited to those of pupils from without. There are, therefore, in every State, large numbers of young persons who have neither fitting opportunities to obtain secondary instruction, nor influences drawing them to seek it. Academies should be organized to meet their wants, as far as this is practicable. These should aim to furnish the best possible training in the English language and literature, in elementary science, and in the modern languages, as well as in the classics and mathematics.

Let me add, as a third reason why preparatory departments can not take the place of academies, that the benefits of the latter would be accessible to young people of both sexes. The day is coming, and that, too, before very long, when the importance of this consideration will be seen in its true light.

These reasons, which show the insufficiency of preparatory departments to do the work which ought to be done, also urge us to the establishment of academies. We need these as centres of quickening influence, both that the people may be more widely and deeply impressed with the value of liberal culture, and that our colleges may be better supplied with students; we need them to furnish secondary education to those for whom no provision is made by existing arrangements; and we need them for the sake of our daughters as well as of our sons.

III. We must ask further in what relation do our high schools stand to this matter? I shall not be understood, in what I am about to say, as failing to recognize the value of the work these schools are doing. It seems to me, however, very clear, that they do not and can not take the place of academies. In the first place, as already shown, they do not occupy the field. Such schools exist only in cities and large towns, and are organized and conducted as local institutions. But, further, very few high schools in the West afford opportunities of classical culture. I have tried to ascertain the number in this State which keep up a classical department, but without success. I have assured myself, however, that the proportion of such schools to the whole number is very small. Even where classical teaching is provided it is generally as a mere appendage to the arrangements of the school, and is so little appreciated that it is very difficult to maintain it regularly and efficiently. High schools therefore are doing very little in this direction.

In the second place such schools do not exert the moral and religious influence which ought to prevail in an academy. We have lately been discussing the question of Bible reading in the public schools. Whether the movement to abolish this is to be successful or not the controversy has put in a clear light the impossibility of giving a decided religious tone to these institutions. No one expects that any longer, and many regard the matter with indifference because it is a fundamental feature of the school system that the children board at home. They therefore enjoy such religious instruction and influences as their parents choose to provide for them. They are also under parental care in respect to habits and conduct out of school. But an academy is necessarily a boarding-school, and towards its pupils it must discharge, in part at least, the duties of a parent. It is therefore not without reason that the organization of such schools is looked upon as a religious enterprise. They ought to be springing up all over the States, working not in hostility to the public schools, but as supplementary to them, and bringing the advantages of liberal culture within the reach of those who live away from the cities, under moral and religious influences which may in some sort supply the place of the associations of home.

But, in the third place, the inevitable tone of the public schools unfit them to do the work of feeders to the colleges. I am sure that there is a widespread misapprehension on this subject. It is difficult for many persons to understand why a school which produces admirable results in certain directions should be disqualified by that very fact from accomplishing certain other results. Yet such is the case, and I think that the more successful our public schools are in their appropriate work, the less will they be fitted to take the place of academies. For one of the most important elements in an institution of learning is the impulse it gives to its pupils. Many schools are almost worthless because they give little or no impulse of any kind. They are mere machines which push the scholars through a certain routine of studies, mills which grind a yearly grist, and often grind it exceedingly fine. But a good school inspires new life in its pupils, gives them new aims and profoundly influences their tastes and inclinations. They are carried along by it with rapid strides in their development of character. What kind of an impulse does it give? In what direction are they borne? These are significant questions. So important have they appeared that it has been questioned whether the effort to carry on scientific in connection with the literary departments of the colleges, is wise. The tone of the two departments must be so diverse. the impulse they seek to give so dissimilar, that it is perhaps a waste of energy to attempt to make them work together. In the college a love of learning for its own sake, enthusiastic study and research for the purpose of culture. for mental growth and expansion of view, ought to be the prevailing sentiment. The old term "humanities." by which literary and classical studies were designated very happily indicated their scope and intent In a school of science on the other hand, there must be equal enthusiasm and thirst for knowledge, but it must be directed always to some practical end; to making skilled chemists, engineers and manufacturers: its scope is narrower and more simple. Both forms of culture are valuable and necessary. but each has methods and tendencies of its own, and each is apt to derogate from the claims and the spirit of the other when they are forced into unnatural union. I think that experience has tended to confirm the wisdom of these views. They have prevailed in France; they are gaining in favor in New England.

It requires no extended statement to show how these considerations affect the fitness of high schools to take the place of academies. The impulse of our public schools must always be towards business life. The principles which have led to their establishment determine this. As already indicated. their mission is to prepare as many of the youth as possible for the intelligent discharge of the duties of citizenship. Moreover, the great majority of the pupils must always tend towards business, and think lightly of culture. These two facts determine the influence of the schools. The tendency will always be to drift men from. rather than towards the colleges. The fourteenth annual report of the public schools of this city says of the high school: "The number of male pupils who complete the classical course with the expectation of entering college, is comparatively small. The large majority of those who enter the school take the studies of the general department. thinking not of professional life, but of business of some kind, the avenues to which are so many and so inviting." The same report shows, out of fifty-seven graduates for the year, only seven from the classical department. In no school in the State are the opportunities for classical study better, or the inducements to enter upon it superior, to those of our high school. Even the establishment of a separate classical school, as a portion of the State system, will not change this tendency. It is inherent in the very nature and constitution of the whole system. The impulse is so fully given in the grammar schools, that few pupils will break away from it and turn themselves towards the classical school. The high school is the natural head and termination of a course; that to which the ambition of the lad points from the beginning, and beyond which he encounters few influences to draw him on Does not this consideration in part explain the fact that during forty-six years ending with 1861 only six hundred pupils entered college from the Boston Latin School; while during only twenty-eight years preceding the same date, more than a thousand entered from Phillips Academy at Andover.

The public schools, then, can not take the place of the academies, because they do not occupy the field, and are not adapted to the want; because they can not exercise the proper religious and moral influence; and because their tone and the impulse they give to their pupils is not of the kind needed for encouraging advanced culture.

IV. Let us, then, proceed further to inquire briefly what are the elements essential to a good academy. They may be summarized thus: Stability, independence, responsibility. The patrons must have assurance that the school is not a mere temporary experiment, an individual enterprise, to be maintained in such ways and for such a time as it can be made financially successful. They must feel in the first place that it is to continue, and steadily to seek the accomplishment of a definite purpose In the second place, they must recognize that the school is above individual caprice and dictation, not compelled to sacrifice right methods, high aims, and strict discipline to catering for patronage. Finally, they must feel that its policy is shaped and directed by competent hands, by whom the teachers are appointed, and to whom they are responsible. In short, an academy must be something more than a mere private school.

One of the first essentials to the establishment of such an institution, therefore, will be an endowment. This need not be large to begin with. I think twenty-five thousand dollars would form a good basis for the foundation of an academy. This fund ought to be increased, with the growth of the school, to four or five times that amount. A library, laboratory, cabinets, etc., could be built up in the course of time. They are all valuable adjuncts to its work, but none of them are vital. I hear very much on this subject with which I have no sympathy. I fear our tendency is to over-estimate the importance of these material accessories of education, fine buildings, cabinets, libraries, etc., and to under-value the importance of life. Men — earnest, able, devoted teachers, with culture and heart and power to give to the work, are, in my view, the most indispensable requisite. They make a school Their value to it is beyond compute, and I would have means provided for paying them, if the school had to be organized in a garret. Depend upon it, fine buildings do not make fine institutions, and as long as we persist in spending our money on brick and mortar instead of on brains,— on chemical retorts and fossil ferns and trilobites instead of on living men,— our progress in educational work will be rather in show than in substance. Let the endowment be, in the beginning, sufficient, with the increase from the school, to secure the services of one or two efficient teachers, and trust to the influence of the school and future efforts in its behalf to provide for its growing wants.

In the second place, an academy must have a properly constituted board of overseers. This is too manifest to need discussion. Besides taking care of its finances and general management, this board ought to provide for stated and competent examinations, that its instruction may be made thorough and progressive

In conclusion, I urge the establishment of academies on the ground that the interests of the Church require this at our hands I fear we are suffering materially from a lack of breadth of view in our educational work. The most absorbing thought in our efforts at present is the training of candidates for the ministry This is the interest which appeals most powerfully and most constantly to the hearts of the Church ; and the need of educated ministers is indeed pressing. But we must be careful that we do not let it stand in our light, and prevent us from seeing both other great necessities and the most effective means of providing for this. An educated laity is hardly less essential to the cause of true religion at the present time than an educated clergy. The various Christian and charitable labors of the Church were never more dependent upon the counsel and efforts of the laity. As teachers, as lecturers, as leaders in science and literature, as legislators, indeed, in all the departments of active life, how essential is it to have intelligent, educated Christian men ! We need a re-awakening on this subject. If we felt its importance as we ought, we should certainly recognize more fully the need of putting in operation the train of causes which will bring as many as possible to obtain a thorough education. If we felt it as we ought, young men of ability and promise in the Churches would be sought out and helped to obtain an education, without exacting from them in advance a pledge that they will enter the ministry.

But even in the narrower view of supplying the pulpits of the denomination, it can hardly be questioned that we are not pursuing the wisest course. When a young man enters an academy, he is generally at the age at which his character first takes its direction, when religious influence is most essential and most likely to produce its legitimate fruits. If we were more active in furnishing the schools needed, in expanding the scope and increasing the patronage of our educational institutions, can it be doubted that, with the blessing of God, we should reap the fruits of our labors in the conversion of many while pursuing their studies? and still further in the turning of many to the work so loudly calling for laborers? We must make a wise use of the means within our reach, we must put in operation the proper train of causes, if we expect to produce the best results. If our colleges are languishing from a lack of organization and breadth of view in our educational work, are not all our interests as a denomination suffering from the same cause? It is a law which even Churches can not afford to overlook, that we shall reap as we sow. If we sow sparingly, we shall reap also sparingly. Have we not sown sparingly, while making our arrangements for a most bounteous harvest? For, see, our educational institutions are strong in proportion as they are farther removed from the people. Our seminaries receive the most favor and attention; our colleges are not wholly overlooked; but our academies — there are no such institutions among us. And yet they should be, as it were, the fallow fields in which to make our abundant sowing. What centres of influence and power they may become! Think of Dr. Arnold's work at the head of Rugby, and the number of men in public life who received their impulse and the mould of their characters from him; or of Dr. Taylor's direction of Phillips Academy at Andover, and its influence in New England and throughout the country, if you would estimate the moral power of a good academy. We must recognize the academy as a necessity and as a source of power, as we never have done, if we expect to infuse new life and strength and progress into our whole system.

The discussion of the paper by Prof. STEARNS was introduced by Prof. JOHN STEVENS of Ohio, who expressed himself as fully endorsing the sentiments of the paper, especially those which related to the pressing demand for academies in the several States.

JUDGE BECK, of Iowa, wished to enter his protest against every sentiment uttered in the paper of Prof. STEARNS. He wished to enter his most decided protest. We do not need academies — at least not denominational academies. Such institutions in Iowa are abortions. The counties in that State are authorized to establish academies, and have done so to a large extent. We can not compete with them. He counselled his brethren of Iowa to support their colleges. If you attempt to establish academies in every county, you will starve both. We are unfortunately divided in Iowa. We are attempting to carry three colleges, which is too much for us, at present; but we hope that we may make a success of them in future. As a denomination, the Baptists did not want to support academies, for such institutions were not purely denominational. The Baptists should support their own denominational colleges and seminaries. For his part he would support no other. And he would say to the Baptists of Iowa, don't give a cent of their money nor a tithe of their time and energies for any educational institutions but those of their own denomination.

Rev. THOMAS BRAND, of Iowa, could not but think that a large portion of the delegates from Iowa would disagree with the last speaker in regard to the establishment of academies. The Baptists of Iowa were in a condition to be benefited by the deliberations of this Convention. We have four institutions which, while they rank merely with academies, bear much more imposing names. If they were only content to be known as academies and do the work of academies, it would be far better for us. What we most need are feeders for our colleges. He referred to the Congregational college at Grinnell, as an instance of the failure of preparatory departments. The professors were looking anxiously for the time when this may be done away with, and academies be established all over the State to prepare students for our colleges. He was, therefore, in favor of the sentiments of the paper read.

Prof. TEN BROEK, of Ann Arbor, thought, if by a resolution of this body we could establish a Rugby or a Phillips Academy, he would be in favor of the sentiments to which he had listened in the paper read before us. But it recommended what everybody knew can never be done. He thought the whole thing impossible, and was opposed to dissipating our strength as low down as the academies. The Union schools of Michigan had done their work admirably well in furnishing students for the State University. He thought we had better complete what we had already begun, rather than attempt impossible things.

Dr. READ, of Minnesota, thought it not wise to carry out the plan proposed in the paper, in the Western States, however well it might work in the old States of the Union. He thought it easier to establish colleges in the West than academies. People in the West were taken by the name university or college, and will give money and lands for establishment and support, while they will not look at a proposal to establish an academy. If only a preparatory department were established at first, it would accomplish all the good claimed for academies, and give an impulse to young men towards a liberal education. The wisest course for us in the West is to concentrate our efforts and our means on institutions already established.

Dr. EVERTS thought the apparent difference on the subject was more on a question of names than anything else. The friends of academies were also the advocates of colleges. He urged that the efforts of the denomination be directed to the securing of their proper share in the control and management of the institutions of learning which are being established by the State, rather than attempt to run counter to them by establishing denominational schools of the same character.

Prof. OLNEY, of Michigan University, had only a few remarks to make. The subject of co-operation with the State system of education was one of vast importance. We do not do well to resign our share of control in the State institutions. The work of preparing students is being done well by the academies of the East. It is being tolerably well done by the high schools of Michigan; but it is not being done at all in the West, except in the preparatory schools of the colleges. The high schools of Michigan feel the influence of the State University, and they are aspiring to prepare students for the University, and consequently they are doing a most excellent preparatory work. The two work together— the University receiving the certificates of qualification in scholarship of the schools. Would it not be well for the colleges of other States to establish the same relations with the high schools ? It would greatly benefit both, and then we should soon have universities in fact as well as in name. The most advanced scholars which enter the University at Ann Arbor come from the high schools.

Rev. A. OWEN, of Michigan, said the expression we have heard from Michigan did not fall in with events. He thought that experience had shown that high schools are not adequate feeders of our colleges, even in that State. Nearly all who graduate from these schools go out into secular life. It is felt that in universities the infidel element exerts an influence altogether disproportionate to its numbers. He thought after the primary school. the State government ought to have little to do with education. We want academies under religious control as feeders of our colleges and universities. He was not in favor of beginning at the top and working downwards in our educational system — that is, establishing colleges first and academies afterwards. After Iowa had taken stand against Iowa in this discussion, it is essential that Michigan should be opposed by Michigan. In Michigan the brethren are hampered by the fact that denominational influence can not prevail over secular power. It can not even compete with it. He spoke in favor of academies. They have a college in Michigan, which suffers because it has no streams to feed it. We should now shape our efforts for the future, and fix the localities for the feeders of the colleges. It was not necessary to have a college in every State.

Prof. STEVENS, of Ohio, spoke decidedly in favor of preparatory departments in colleges. They were an absolute necessity in the present condition of things in that State.

Rev. J. V. SCHOFIELD, of Iowa, thought his friend (Judge Beck) had mistaken a secular academy for one under religious influence, as proposed in the paper. He had established one of the former, and it had gone to pieces, as was quite natural. Nor did he agree with Dr. Read, that we should establish the college, and wait for the academy, as an offshoot or outgrowth of it. He opposed schools where they were afraid to read the Bible. He favored learning and religion. In many parts of Iowa colleges were languishing. Public schools alone could not be sufficient to feed the higher institutions. There was a necessity for academies, under the control of the Baptist denomination.

Rev. E. A. GASTMAN, Superintendent of Public Schools in Decatur, Illinois, indorsed some of the views presented in the paper read. On the subject of academies he thought there was a difference of opinion. With many of the sentiments of the paper he heartily agreed. But he opposed the establishing of academies by the denomination, so generally as recommended, for the reason that the Baptists could not sustain them as distinctively denominational institutions. He referred to numerous failures where the experiment had been tried. He thought the reason why young men went out from our high schools into business was not owing to the want of academies, but to the intense activity of the age. He did not think that the increase of academies would remedy this evil. The common school system, he was aware, was not perfect; yet through the high schools it was doing much to recruit and keep up our colleges.

Rev. Dr. MARSENA STONE, of Ohio, said, whatever may have been the success of high schools in Michigan, as feeders of the colleges, they had utterly failed in Ohio. The difficulty is that those who have control of our high schools in Ohio are not only indifferent but generally opposed to classical studies. In that State there is a majority for academies, for preparatory schools *as* preparatory schools. It is impossible in his State to fit students for college in the common or high schools. It was seldom that good men would assume the duties of school trustees, and whenever classical studies were introduced, they would not be continued for more than a year before other trustees would be elected in opposition to such a course, and thus the student preparing for college would be thrown out.

2

Rev. Dr. PATTISON, of Chicago, spoke from forty years experience as an educator. He thought the subject of academics was one of great importance. We must have more college students. He meant college students in a proper sense, not preparatory students. The preparatory schools of the colleges were almost the only source of supply of college students in this country. But these schools had a depressing influence upon the college course, for one reason, that they so largely outnumbered the regular students. He thought that if Iowa were to establish academics throughout the State, in ten years a majority of them would be empty. He thought it better to have three or four well-endowed academics or colleges — whichever we might name them — in that State, than to attempt so general a system as had been suggested. We can not sustain Baptist colleges without Baptist nurseries, which we could not expect to have in the general high schools of the country. They were sought by young men who cared only for a secular education — an education to prepare them for business, for making money, and not those who had aspirations after learning, for learning's sake.

The following paper was then read by Rev. H. L. Wayland, D.D., President of Franklin College, Indiana, upon

THE QUESTION OF THE EDUCATION OF THE WOMEN OF THE WEST, INCLUDING THAT OF THE ADMISSION OF BOTH SEXES TO THE SAME INSTITUTIONS OF HIGHER LEARNING.

I retain enough of the traditions of a military life, to know that it would be a violation of all the Articles of War and of all the Army Regulations, for a subordinate to urge his own incompetence as a reason for declining to execute the order of his superior officer. And so, when the general of our peaceful army, whose commission is the Baptist Educational Commission, bade me attempt this subject, I obeyed without gain-saying, though I was as well aware as you can be, of the moment and delicacy of the questions involved, and of the impossibility of giving them due consideration in the scanty and weary hours left from the task of creating the means of existence for a feeble and struggling college.

The subject naturally presents itself under three heads:

I. The Education of Women, considered at large;

II. The Education of the Women of the West;

III. The question of the joint education of the two sexes, in our higher institutions.

I. Of the Education of Women, considered at large:

Shall women have as good an education as is enjoyed by men? I employ the term Education for the sake of brevity. I mean, of course, shall they have as good *opportunities* of education? *We* are responsible for giving women *opportunities*. *Education* depends on themselves, and their use of the opportunities. But I presume that I run no risk of being misunderstood when I ask: Shall women have as good an education as is enjoyed by men?

Yes, and, first, on the ground of *justice*. Woman is a human being, and so, entitled to all the rights inherited by any human being. We may venture to reckon this as a self-evident principle.

If any one should assert that women are by nature inferior to men in mental endowment, and therefore are not competent to use, and therefore can not claim, equal opportunities, I think the burden of proof would rest against him who made the assertion, and we may defer any disproof, till something more than assertion is adduced.

If indeed it should be alleged that women have not *shown* themselves the equals of men in achievement, that, of the great triumphs won by mankind, the vast preponderance has been due to men, and an almost infinitesimal proportion to women, may not a sufficient reply be found in the fact, that men, with a selfishness truly masculine, have usurped all the opportunities; that women, destitute, on the one hand of the cultivated powers coming from a large education, have, on the other hand, been without avenues to greatness and without the stimulus which the existence of these avenues would have imparted?

Were not the preternatural achievements of the army of Marengo and of Austerlitz due largely to the principle announced by their leader, "the career open to genius," and to the apothegm, "every French soldier carries a marshal's baton in his knapsack?" Are not the limited attainments and achievements of woman explained by the want of possibilities, the absence of a career?

The enlistment of the Baptist women of America in the work of Foreign Missions, just inaugurated, is to be hailed with gratitude, not only for the blessings that will result to the heathen, but equally for the reflex influence upon our own women, providing for them a great object, and a worthy employment for powers that have so often been wasted in idleness, or have toiled ingloriously in the service of fashion and of interests most contemptible.

But, after all, the question scarcely demands discussion. Let both sexes be treated with absolute justice, in the matter of education, both be allowed equal advantages, both be subjected to the same demands, and very soon the feebler, the less capable will fall behind and disappear from the competition. The question will settle itself.

Surely, on the ground of justice, women are entitled to as good an opportunity of education as men.

And if there is to be any discrimination, the same justice would indicate that it should be in favor of women.

First, because they suffer under so many difficulties, that they require some compensating advantage to place them on a level. While men are possessed of superior physical strength, and hold in their hands the vast preponderance of wealth, and wield the law-making power in their own behalf, it certainly appears that women, in order to have any show for a fair chance, need the mental and moral force derived from a large and true education.

Every one must have remarked that women possessed of high intelligence and education, find themselves no more than able to hold their own, in the varied relations which they sustain to men, often vastly their inferiors in everything but in the advantages given them by the constitution of society. But for the possession of the faculties derived from high culture, Mrs. Butler and Mrs. Norton would have truly been objects of pity.

Second, the discrimination should be made in favor of woman, because man finds, as she does not, an *education* in the very circumstances and necessities of his life. A husband and a wife were, at the time of their marriage, equals in education and in intellectul activity. Compare them now, after twenty years. The man has mingled with his fellows, in business, trade, politics, legislation; has bought and sold, lost money, made money, cheated and been cheated, has served in the militia, and been out in the three months, has exhorted in religious meetings, has attended caucusses, and made nominations, has had his mind exercised in hearing and weighing the arguments adduced by the ablest political speakers of the State; has been on the School Committee, has been elected to the Legislature, has run for Congress, and in common with every adult male citizen of the United States, has expected to be president Though-ignorant of books, he is, in some sense, an educated man, possessor of himself, a person, whom, though you do not love, you can not ignore.

And his wife? She has baked, and ironed, taken the baby to meeting, and entered the Kingdom of Heaven at odd spells. Possibly she has given and attended tea-parties, and been Treasurer of the Sewing Society. And the world says: "Dear me! How could Gen. Blank marry such a commonplace woman?"

Not long ago an intelligent man said to me: "If I had two sons, one of whom was to be a professional man, and the other a mechanic or tradesman, and if I should make any distinction between them, I would give the better education to the latter. because the former would soon acquire an education in the very practice of his calling." The sentiment is not without an element of justice and at any rate is useful as a corrective of an injurious excess in an opposite direction. I apprehend that the same principle may find application to the matter now under review.

In the long run, the most impartial justice is always promotive of the largest good. And then, I am led to remark that a regard for the *general welfare* demands the equal education of women It is not, and can not be, for the good of society at large. that any portion of it should be hampered and crippled. No part of the race can attain its development, while any part lags. The right side can not be in health, while the left is dwarfed. Assuredly women have. even more lamentably than men, failed of the divinely appointed destiny. And in this failure, have we not all been kindred? Has not the injustice avenged itself, by the lowered tone imparted to society, by the feeble mental and spiritual life transmitted to the coming generation?

There is, I believe, in woman, a wealth of nature. a power of aspiration, attainment, and achievement, now lying dormant, that needs only opportunity and inspiration to awake to conscious existence. And who can tell how vastly the riches, the happiness, the elevation and glory of humanity will be enhanced, when these. now undeveloped resources shall be called into activity? Truly. "if one member suffers all the members suffer with it, if one member be honored all the members rejoice with it."

What then? Granting that women are to have an equal education with men, shall they have just the same education? Not necessarily. I do not think that every woman should have just the same education as every man, nor every man the same as every other man, nor every woman as every other woman. The Deity has not made any two leaves, any two blades of grass, any two flowers, exactly similar. No two faces are precise duplicates. Shall we suppose that He has so constructed *minds*, that every one shall be an absolute repetition of every other?

> "No compound of this earthly ball
> Is like another, all in all."

And diverse as are the minds of men, so diverse are their destinies.

The education, then, suited to each person would seem to be the one which will enable him to use to the best advantage his native powers so as to attain in the highest degree to the destiny which God and nature assigned him. It would appear, that to no two persons is there precisely the same education, that there is no one absolute education, any more than there is one absolute rainbow, but rather, as many as there are persons.

To the question then, Shall we give to women and to men the self-same education? I answer, not necessarily the same, but on the same principles. I would not create one education and say, "this is for men," and then another and say, " this is for women." I would provide for all, for men, for women, the largest and widest facilities of choice, and then I would say to every one, be it man or woman, "consider your own constitution; consider the work to which you are led by your inward character and your outward surroundings. And, whatever is the utterance of the divine voice to you, whether it say: be an artist; be a statesman; be a linguist; be a naturalist; be a tourist; be a preacher; be a house-keeper; be a trader; heed and follow this voice.

You understand that I am now speaking, not of primary scholars, not of babies at the breast, but of young *women* in our higher institutions, young women corresponding to the young men in our colleges, as I am advised that they are sometimes compared with them.

Is it said they may choose unwisely? But is it any more true here, than everywhere else in life? They may choose unwisely in religion, in employment, in marriage; but shall we therefore take from them the power of choice?

I learn with pleasure from my valued friend, Dr. Gregory, of the Illinois Industrial University, an Institution whose brief past has been eminently glorious and which promises to achieve a future even more splendid, that the Faculty of Instruction have arranged six courses of study and that they say to each pupil, male or female, "Unless you have some reason to the contrary, we advise you to select and follow some one of these. But you are not restricted. You may make up a course containing parts of two or more. You may select any that you please of the branches here pursued."

II. We are next to consider the education of the women of the West. And here I profess myself a little at a loss. I take the topic as it is given me; yet I am not sure that I plainly see wherein the education required for the women of the West differs from that demanded for their sisters of the East, save in this: that it is similar to that for the women of the East, only *more so.*

Should not the education of the women of the West be,

1st An education of *powers* rather than *accomplishments?* Is it not one of the crying sins of our female education that it gives so much time to mere accomplishments? Thousands of young women are spending from two to seven hours daily for five, or perhaps ten, successive years upon the piano, and kindred instruments of torture. Nor do they intend this as a means of subsistence. If so, their perseverance would be praiseworthy. It is to them an accomplishment, pure and simple. So of the time given to drawing, painting and other ornamental branches. Let me not be misunderstood. If a person has a natural bent for any one of these pursuits, or if circumstances point it out as his means of gaining a livelihood, or of conferring pleasure upon himself or his friends, it is well. Nor do I object to these branches being pursued, in moderation, by persons even who have no special genius for them. No doubt it would be for the benefit of us all, men and women, to understand something of the rudiments of music, as also of the laws of outline and color. It would enable us, in a higher degree, to appreciate the sounds and the aspects of nature.

But I object to the excessive time devoted to these branches by those who have no aptitude for them, who will make no use of them and who will shed all these fine feathers immediately after pairing.

I have no acquaintance with these matters myself, but I have been told by persons versed in music that they find in it but a very slight discipline and improvement of the mental faculties.

And the value of these accomplishments is largely *incidental.* They are greatly dependent upon accidental circumstances, for the power to give pleasure to one's self or to others. So long as pianos are in fashion, and so long as a person has one at hand, the power of performing upon it may be useful. But it is not always that one has a piano. There are a great many circumstances in life where skill in the use of this instrument would be absolutely worthless.

But the power of reasoning, the power of generalizing, the power of gaining knowledge from books or from nature,—it is not possible to conceive of a position where these powers will not be in the highest degree useful and beneficent. At the head of a prosperous family, or in poverty and widowhood, amid society or in loneliness, in youth and attractiveness, or in old age, amid civilization and outside its bounds, she who is possessed of these powers can hardly fail to convey pleasure and to confer benefits.

2. It should be an education of *character* rather than of *acquisitions.* It is a good thing to *know* Spanish, German, French, Latin, Greek, the sciences, history and music. It is a better thing to *be* a woman, well-balanced, master of her own resources, calm, prudent, inventive, resolute, self-reliant, hospitable to ideas and sentiments, so pure, so large, so high, as to command reverence, fulfilling that lofty ideal, so familiar that I beg pardon for quoting it, so just that it can nardly be quoted too often :

> " A being breathing thoughtful breath ;
> A traveler between life and death ;
> The reason firm, the temperate will ;
> Endurance, foresight, strength and skill ;
> A perfect woman, nobly planned,
> To guide, to counsel and command ;
> And yet a spirit too, and bright
> With something of an angel light."

" I AM " was the lofty designation by which the Deity chose to reveal Himself to mankind. And I would have the women of the West so educated that they shall say " I am " rather than " I know."

3. The education of the women of the West should be one that will continue through life Women pursue various studies and make fair proficiency in them. Then they drop them for aye, and languages, science and music seem like a dream of childhood to the woman who has been married ten years. But is it not possible to impart to them an education that shall be so far in accordance with the demands and pursuits of their lives as to be carried on ? And if there are two educations, whereof the one is sure to be very early discontinued, while the other, possessing equal disciplinary value in the present, has a prospect of being carried forward through life, shall we not prefer the latter ? Physiology, organic chemistry, hygiene,—surely the daily experience of every mother and housewife ought to keep these studies bright by use. And so of intellectual philosophy. It has often been said that if any one could observe and record the history of his own mind

and its gradual unfoldings, he would write the most valuable treatise on metaphysics ever produced. But who has a better opportunity than the mother to know the genesis of the mind? Is it not to the nursery and to the observations of the mother that we must look for the facts that shall lie at the foundation of a true educational philosophy? And who has more need to know the principles of ethics and to be able to apply them than the mother, called upon to decide a thousand questions of right, for her little kingdom, and often compelled to be a conscience to her husband?

4. The education of the women of the West ought to be one that shall induce in them *independence* rather than the reverse, *dependence;*— does not this one word express the state of our women? Dependent, before marriage, upon their fathers, after marriage, upon their husbands; dependent upon Mrs. Grundy for their opinions and rules of conduct, dependent upon the courtesans of Paris for their manner of dress, dependent upon Bridget for their daily bread; dependent because of their ignorance of the world, their ignorance of the laws affecting themselves, their children, their property, their ignorance of the commonest things. And this dependence, is it accidental? Is it not rather the result toward which their education has purposely tended? In 1858, Dr. Nott, in reply to enquiries addressed to him by the regents of the University of Michigan, touching the proposed co-education of the two sexes in that Institution, wrote: "A difference of sex and of destination through the entire journey of life, has, in the judgment of mankind, been thought to require a difference in the distinctive attributes to be called into exercise, and the peculiar type of character to be formed. Delicacy of sentiment, a *feeling of dependence*, and shrinking from the public view, are attributes sought for in the one sex; in the other, decision of character, self-reliance, a feeling of personal independence and a willingness to meet opposition and encounter difficulties " Surely, if it was the design of our system of education to produce in woman a feeling and a condition of dependence, the experiment has been a glorious success. But, despite the sincere veneration I feel for the memory of the Nestor of American instructors; despite, also, the unutterable pangs which it costs me even to differ in opinion from any human being, I must express my opinion that dependence is not a thing to be cultivated, but rather that women, no less than men, should be self-reliant, forceful, in a word, independent, and that our education should have this aim. It should create in woman an aspiration for independence, a sense of its dignity a sense of the humiliation ever attendant upon voluntary vassalage; a conviction that " to be weak is to be miserable." It should give to her the power of achieving an independence. It should give her an industry, a means of support. It should teach her her rights, and should enable her to maintain them. It should teach her to judge, to reason, to form her own opinions, and to rely upon them. Let her begin to do something for her own support when she attains to womanhood, reckoning it unworthy of herself, as she would deem it unworthy of her brother, to remain a pensioner on her father. Let her be prepared to maintain herself, whether she chance to find a husband, or not Let her not be forced to accept of any offer, however distasteful, for the sake of a home, saying, " Put me into one of the priest's offices, (the priestship of wifehood and maternity,) that I may eat but a morsel of bread." Let her be mistress in her own house, able to rule it, able to hold in control her domestic forces, or, if need be, to dispense with them. I think I have heard that on the 4th of July, 1776, our fathers declared themselves independent of England. How happy shall we be, if, by a century later, their daughters shall be independent of Ireland. And

this independence, I think that a true education can do much to create and foster. For example, in regard to her own household, a woman truly educated will have her own faculties perfectly in hand, so that she can bring them to bear on her household work, in the best way and in the shortest time, making it perceptible that even in these ordinary material concerns there is a difference, and that *mind* tells in keeping house as in commanding an army and in writing a poem. A woman truly educated would discover the difference between the real and the unreal, between the essentials of comfort and the demands of fashion, and would reduce the labors of the house by emancipating herself from many enslaving burdens. If she should have company, she would have fewer pies and jellies, but more heart and brains and tongue. If she has servants, she will herself be at the head of the house, wielding the supremacy to which she is entitled by virtue of her character, her manifest superiority. One reason why the domestic does not acknowledge the superiority of the lady of the house, is, because there is no superiority to acknowledge, except in the accident of birth and position.

I do not affirm that such an education as I have feebly described, would be out of place at the East. I am sure that it is demanded for the women of the West. ·

There remains but the question,

III. Shall the two sexes be educated together in our higher institutions of learning?

Permit me to say that I regard this as eminently an open question. While I shall offer such remarks as have occurred to me, I am well aware that many instructors, entitled to far more consideration than myself, have been led, by weighty arguments, to a different conclusion. I can but present the matter as it appears to me.

What is our design in the education of the two sexes? If the opinion lately cited from Dr. Nott is granted, his conclusion would seem inevitable. If we want to produce in men and in women characters utterly diverse, to cherish as virtues in the one sex what we repress as vices in the other, then surely he is right in deciding against co-education ; for, as he justly observes, " it is not easy to see how appliances for the production of such opposite results can be furnished by the same agencies, at the same time, and in the same place."

But shall we grant the premises? Is it our design to .produce in woman a character all softness, gentleness, guilelessness, tenderness, modesty, purity, ignorance of ill, and to create in man a character all wisdom, strength, force, might, self-reliance, boldness in attempting, pride in achieving, awed by no obstacles, withheld by no restraints? Did Grace Darling and Florence Nightingale, and Dorothy L. Dix and Deborah, the prophetess, violate the proprieties of the one sex, when they faced obstacles, underwent dangers, exhibited self-reliance, and did not shrink from public observation? And was Napoleon less a man when he shed a tear at the sight of a dog watching by the body of his slain master?

Closely allied to this notion of a male and a female character is that of a male and a female standard of servitude. A man may be sensual, overbearing, unscrupulous, unfeeling, provided only he is not wanting in *courage.* A woman may be cowardly, ignorant, insufficient, indolent, deceitful, provided only she retain what the world calls virtue, and provided she has no opinion — or, at any rate, carefully conceals this possession. A man may violate the seventh commandment, and be the idol of the nation, as was Admiral Nelson. A woman! ——

Are there, then, two standards of rectitude? Are there two decalogues? Are there with us, as with the heathen, two classes of deities, male and female, given as models for the two sexes respectively? Or have we rather *one* perfect type and exemplar, who has given us an example that we should follow in his steps, and in whom is neither male nor female? Is Christ divided, and shall the one sex take His courage and His self-reliance, while the other appropriates His purity and His tenderness? Is there any trait that is noble in the one sex that is not admirable in the other as well?

It being understood, then, that we do not wish, as the result of education, to produce diverse and opposite traits of character; that we regard no virtue as being the property of either sex alone, no vice as being tolerable in either, and that we shall secure the best results by letting not only each sex, but each human being of whatever sex, reach the highest development possible on the line which God has indicated, permit me to remark :

1. Co-education seems the system approved by *nature*. The sexes are associated in families during youth, and the invariable experience is that those are the noblest women and those the most lovely men who grow up in a house where are both brothers and sisters. The sexes are together in the earlier part of their education, and I think I have observed a tendency on the part of the two to become closely associated during the period of maturer life. The drift of nature is unmistakable, and we are entitled to ask — Why should the few years of the higher education be an exception?

2. Joint education is commended on the ground of a true *economy*. I suppose that almost any one of our higher institutions of learning could educate twice the number of its present pupils with but slight additional expense. Let us suppose, in any one of our States, a college, whose entire property represents from $200.000 to $500.000. It is open to young men only. Now what provision shall be made for young women? I see but three possible courses. We may found, at equal expense, a college for them; we may give them an inferior education; or we may, with slight additional expenditure, throw open the first-named institution to both sexes.

It is true, economy is not the only, nor the leading, consideration. There is money enough to supply all the necessities of God's cause; but we ought not to squander it. The same voice that bade the loaves multiply to the demands of the hour, also bade the disciples "gather up the fragments,"

Perhaps it would be more just to say that, under the system of co-education we can make our means effective of greater good. Having a given amount of resources in money and in competent instructors, we can produce *one* institution for both sexes, that shall be an honor to the cause of Christian education, the success of which shall encourage and enlarge the liber-ality and the holy enterprise of the people of God. This is a true, a far-sighted economy.

3. There is on the part of each of the sexes a strong desire to secure the approbation of the other. Men have wrought brave deeds to gain the smile of women, and women make great sacrifices to win the admiration of men. Will not the association of the two sexes in study, and the desire on the part of each to excel in presence of the other, prove a powerful stimulant to mental exertion?

This union of the two sexes will naturally lead to the employment of the members of both sexes as teachers in our higher institutions. As a result there will be opened before female teachers an avenue that will quicken their aspirations, and there will also, perhaps, arise a degree of generous emulation between the members of the two sexes thus associated in the same noble calling. In this, as in every similar contest between them, may the one keep perpetually in advance, and the other perpetually overtake and outstrip it.

4. Each of the sexes is naturally disposed to treat the other with more of deference than it pays to its own members. Women feel this in presence of men, and men are proverbially respectful in presence of females. The vilest hesitate to swear before a woman. Will not this instinctive and mutual feeling of deference engender a refinement of manners, a cultivation among those who are educated together?

5. Will not the educating young men and young women in the same institution and in the same classes promote the greater happiness of each in the relations of future life? Scarcely anything makes or mars the happiness of a man more than marriage — and of the woman this is even more true; and yet there are so many wretched marriages that the successes are the exception. And *educated* persons are by no means exempted, as would appear from the general belief that women of genius are apt to marry dunces, and that men of genius have a kindred liability.

And why? After making due allowance for many other causes, is it not largely due to the fact that men marry knowing little or nothing of the women they marry and as little of the sex at large, and that women marry in a state of equal ignorance? A young man, studious in his habits, retiring in his disposition, has spent five or ten years in comparative seclusion. He has read every book except one — the book of human nature, in two volumes, and he is especially ignorant of volume two. He enters the world; he goes into society; he is dazzled — fascinated. He thinks every woman an angel, and only wonders where are her wings. He falls in love, of course; — he marries. It is all a lottery. The same Providence that watches over children and drunken men may watch over him, and he may build wiser than he knows. But then, again, he may not. He may marry an economical housekeeper, who will mend his clothes and see to the kitchen. He may marry a neat, well-dressed nonentity — a bundle of negatives.

And the woman — is her danger any less? She enters life imagining that every man is a Bayard, without fear and without reproach; that every divine is — divine, and so on. And presently she is married. She does not always find her fancies confirmed by experience. Even if the persons thus united are good in themselves, yet, if they are unsuited, mismated, it is a failure, no less.

Now, let us suppose that, for several years, these persons had been in the same institution, had recited in the same classes; they would have measured each other, they would have learned each other's faults and weaknesses, they would have seen and heard each other's failures and mortifications, they would have become dis-illusioned. Perhaps the irrevocable step would have been deferred, or, if an early engagement were formed, it would certainly be more judicious than if contracted between persons ignorant each of the other and of the sex whereof the other is a member. Such might be presumed, I think, to be the results of joint education. And has not experience justified the expectation? The experiment (for it has not ceased to be an experiment) has been successful where it has been fairly tried. Nor do I know of any institution in which joint education has obtained where a backward step has been taken. But no institution must think its duty done when it has opened its doors and has invited woman to repair thither. There must be suitable facilities; chiefly, there must be a lodging and boarding hall for the Female Department, with suitable parlors, etc., where the social influences shall be under the wise guidance of judicious teachers.

But there are objections to joint education. Of course, there are objections to everything that is proposed, except, perhaps, to the annexation of San Domingo. For example, there is urged the danger to morality. But is the danger annihilated, or even lessened, by separate education? I think that more scandal transpires in connexion with separate institutions than with the reverse. The nations that have most strenuously practiced the seclusion of women, and the separation of the sexes, have not been distinguished for eminent purity. Grant that there is temptation. But life is a series of temptations, and education consists not so much in perfectly secluding the young from them, as in teaching them to recognize, to combat, to conquer them. Or do you say that by co-educating we are in danger of obliterating the distinctive marks which characterise the two sexes, which rescue humanity from a tedious monotony render the society of either sex so attractive to the members of the other? But do women educated with men cease to be women? Do men at large lose the distinctive features of their character by association with each other? If Michael Angelo, Isaac Newton, Arthur Wellesley, James Watt, William Wordsworth, Napoleon Bonaparte and Daniel Boone had been educated in the same school, do you imagine that no difference of character would remain in them? Do I need to add that for women, as for men, it is a Christian education that is needed, an education whose motives are drawn from the word of God, an education that sets before each pupil, as the highest destiny, a life of service to God and humanity, a life conformed to the example of the man of Nazareth and of Calvary and informed by his Spirit?

When woman shall be enlightened, enfranchised, transfigured by a true education; when there shall lie open before her avenues to eminence, possibilities that shall be an inspiration; when she shall fulfill the destiny of inward attainment, of outward achievement, for which God created her, then need we no longer look to the far-off future for the age of gold, promised by poet and prophet. Already the Eastern sky will be streaked with the dawning of the Millennium.

After the reading of the paper the Convention adjourned with prayer by Rev. Dr. Pattison, of Illinois.

AFTERNOON SESSION.

2, P. M.

The session was opened with prayer by Rev. D. P. Smith, D.D., of Iowa.

The subject of the morning paper was taken up and discussed.

Rev. Dr. CUTTING was the first speaker. He regarded the subject as one of very grave importance, and one that should awaken particular attention among the Baptists. The questions were practical ones to every person who had to educate his daughter. We could not determine upon the capacity of the sexes whether they should be educated together or not. They were sometimes compelled to educate them together, and there was a disposition

in other places to try the experiment thoroughly. The venture
would be according to the regulations of the institution. If they
were brought into social relations there would be large numbers of
matrimonial alliances as the result. There might be special guard-
ianships, and under those would be the safety. He doubted if it
were desirable to unite the sexes in their education. He had seen
marks of the influence of female minds on students who came to
college. We should know in the future, and the question would
be settled. The whole subject is undergoing a pretty thorough
discussion before the public, and if argument can bring us to a
sound and safe conclusion, we shall undoubtedly reach one at an
early period.

Prof. STEVENS, of Denison University, followed. He said
he was a graduate of a college where the students took off all the
girls in town worth taking. There was one he would have carried
off had he not known her mother. The male and female colleges
were not united — at Oberlin the sexes were separate and under
different teachers. He did not see any danger from the intercourse
spoken of. He approved the sentiments of the paper, thinking
them eminently wise. They are not extreme, one way or the other,
but are characterized by moderation and great good sense. He
was unable to appreciate the objections which the opponents of the
admission of women to our colleges urge against the measure.
They are more a matter of prejudice than of fact or reason.

Judge BECK, of Iowa, spoke in favor of extending the same
educational facilities to women as to men. Without doubt the
women of to-day are as highly educated as their husbands who are
farmers and mechanics. If women were to be lawyers, professors,
physicians, etc., they should be educated accordingly. If she
discharged her mission in this world, she would be married before
she was thirty, and she would become ver y well educated by that
time. He would educate the girls with the girls, and the boys
with the boys. The standard of scholarship in mixed schools is
not as high as in schools where the sexes are separated. The right
of suffrage would probably be conferred on woman, but whether she
received it or not, she should be educated for the sphere in which
she was to move, and Latin and Greek would be of little practical
use to her. Yet as a means of mental discipline they undoubtedly
would serve a valuable purpose.

Prof. SHEPHARDSON spoke to the same effect. If there were
any truth in the commonly received opinion that "woman was the
divinely-appointed teacher of the race," he wanted to see woman
educated in some way. She must have it. The East had done
nothing scarcely for the education of women, and the West should

take hold of the matter and give them a chance. The sentiment that she should be as fully and thoroughly educated as man is rapidly gaining ground among our people, and he thought that old prejudices on this subject would soon give way to a more enlightened feeling than had hitherto prevailed.

Prof. TEN BROEK, of Michigan University, remarked that he had in his experience generally found women apt to teach. Many excelled as teachers. And it is not an uncommon thing, for the female part of the family to receive better education than the males. Aside from the professions, the women were educated as well, if not better than the men. After going to a certain extent in these reforms we should fight against nature, and the women would never get into politics much — a woman would never be President.

Prof. JEWETT, of Milwaukee, wished to hear from some one who had had experience in educating the sexes together. There was nothing like experience as tests for questions like this.

Prof. CURRIER, of Iowa, replied that the results had been entirely satisfactory wherever the experiment had been tried. The students were none the less manly or womanly; nor were they less scholarly. So far as his experience went, the girls stood as high in the classes as the boys. He saw no objections to the new policy, but everything in its favor.

Rev. THOMAS BRAND, of Iowa, said that the experience of the college at Grinnell had been equally satisfactory. The plan had worked well.

Rev. D. H. COOLEY, of Iowa, said that so far as the Lawrence University at Appleton, Wis., is concerned, the average lady graduates were superior to the males, and there had not been the slightest trouble arising from the admission of both sexes.

Rev. Dr. ALLEN, of Minnesota, could indorse all that had been said on this point. He was decidedly in favor of educating the sexes together. The experiment had even turned out better than its friends anticipated.

The Convention then listened to a paper by Rev. Sampson Talbot, D.D., President of Denison University, Ohio, upon

THE PLACE OF SCIENTIFIC STUDIES IN PRESENT EDUCATION.

If the so-called "New Education" is really a higher education, the world needs to know it; for the intellectual forces of a nation determine the grade of its civilization, no less than its philosophy and its morals. Certain it is that there is an increasing dissatisfaction in the public mind with the present modes of education. The origin of this dissatisfaction is to be sought, partly, no doubt, in that restless, revolutionary spirit now abroad, which is

opposed to everything existing just because it exists, and would make all
things new out of—it yet knows not what. The summons to reform is
sometimes only a summons to destroy. It may proceed, in part, also, from
changed conditions, and be able to justify itself by appeal to actual serious
defects in the present education. The demand for reform has at least thus
far made good its claim to have a hearing. The reform demanded is briefly
this: that the Modern Sciences shall take the place of much of the old
learning; in particular, that the Greek and Latin shall give way to modern
languages and special studies.

The topic assigned me may be treated specifically, as the place of Scientific
Studies in present collegiate education, or, more comprehensively, the place
of these studies in general education. As answering best what I conceive
to be the needs of the present occasion, I shall first consider the subject in
its wider applications, taking the different branches of study in their general
relations; and next seek to determine the place of Scientific Studies in the
present college system of this country. The terms Science and Scientific,
unless otherwise qualified, will be understood to refer in accordance with
common usage to the physical sciences. It may be necessary, in order to
guard against any possible misunderstanding, to remark at the outset, that
if this paper shall assume somewhat the form of a polemic, it should be
ascribed to the exclusive claims set up by some in behalf of the study of
Science, not to any intention to depreciate the true value of Science, as an
instrument of education. What, then, is the relation of these sciences to
other branches of education?

The physical sciences are in some respects quite subordinate. They are
inferior, in the first place, to metaphysics. They are occupied with the
finite and the conditioned, and their methods are not applicable beyond
these. The sphere of their movement is the closed circle of secondary
causes, and they can not embrace in their view either absolute beginnings
or absolute endings, or, indeed, independent existence of any kind. They
never can rise to the conception of a just cause, nor of the true infinite.
Hence they are not competent to speak on the question of the existence of
God, or the mode of His connection with nature, of an original act of creation, of final causes, of the possibility of a revelation, or, in general, of the
supernatural. They can not, in fact, account ultimately for anything; they
can not give all the reasons why anything is at all, or why it is as it is.
They have to take things just as they find them, and operate only in the
sphere of the dependent. The field and the method of the natural sciences,
therefore, definitely exclude them from the field and the method of metaphysics; and those who affect to despise metaphysics in the interests of
positive science would do well to consider the limitations which they impose
upon themselves. It is quite possible that a little metaphysics would be a
healthful propædeutic to some of the scientific theorists of our times. We
should at any rate hear less of physical science as an adequate interpreter
of nature and as about to present us with the final explanation of the
universe. Not even evolution can dispense with creation, nor natural selection with final causes; for a philosophy of development is not a philosophy
of origin, and progress by selection does not carry itself on without any
ultimate principle or reason of the movement. No process in things already
existing can dispense with the act which gave them existence, nor can the
process account for itself, nor eliminate from itself the intelligence which
originated it and guides it to its end. The natural sciences, then, can never
construct a philosophy of nature, for two reasons; first, because they find

ERRATA.

Page 30, twenty-third line from the bottom, for "just cause," read "first cause."

Page 31, twelfth line from the bottom, for "painful periods," read "fruitful periods." Nineteenth line from the bottom, for "of literature," read "to literature."

Page 33, twenty-eighth line from the bottom, for "reforming," read "informing."

all their material. their principles, forces and laws, already existent, and have to begin with these as given; and, secondly, because nature itself is nothing to the man of science until he *thinks* it, that is, interprets it, not by his senses, not by experience, but by thought. Nature as such embraces only the manifold of objects; its unity, its laws, man finds in his own reason. The outer world knows no difference between the one and the many, knows nothing of number, nothing of genera and species, of substance and attribute; but these are intellectual elements, they are thoughts. Mind is a deeper fact than matter; thought is the only interpreter and the only principle of the universe. Hence philosophy is superior to science and gives to the sciences their eyes and their light and their seeing.

Nor, in the second place, can the sciences be substituted for mathematics in any system of education. No one, we suppose, claims that they can. Mathematics has a distinct field and method of its own. It treats of the relations of quantity in space and of number in time, while the sciences treat of the objects themselves and of the relations of their parts in organisms. As to method, mathematics is a purely abstract science, with the single relation of equality between its terms, and hence is throughout analytical. It is this which gives to mathematics its accuracy and universality. All its elements are placed together in their simplest state, so that the truth of every relation affirmed may become self-evident. The sciences, on the contrary, deal with concrete objects, standing in various relations to one another, and their method is one of induction and synthesis. Further, mathematics enters more or less into the basis of all the sciences. Nothing physical exists which does not have elements that are mathematical. The law of the correlation of forces brings all the parts of nature into definite relations. And though this law becomes less obvious and less important as we ascend higher, it may not be too much to anticipate that even those sciences which converse with organized and living forms may yet be classed among the exact sciences. Mathematics is then of necessity a first study, a preparatory for all the sciences. How far it should be carried in a system of education will be considered further on.

In the third place, can scientific studies take the place of the study of language? Language lies next to mind; it is the immediate incarnation of thought. The study of language is the introduction of literature, history, and philosophy, and thence to the social and political sciences. All the learning and wisdom of the race, all the accumulated experiences of the past, are borne down to us on the stream of language; by it man comes into connection with the whole vast organism known as humanity. Without it, he would be chiefly limited to the sphere of his own senses: without it, there would be no history and the world would not constitute a community. And since some of the most painful periods in the history of our race, the germinal and formative eras, are hidden from the present in tongues which have ceased to be spoken, they can be summoned before the student in living forms only by acquaintance with these languages. It is evident, then, that the sciences can never take the place of this study.

Can they, in the fourth place, be substituted for those studies which have for their subject the human mind? But they do not explore this realm at all, the most productive, the nearest of all to us. Man will never cease to be interested in himself; the mental sciences will continue to engage his attention. Logic, psychology, and moral philosophy, reveal man to himself and declare to him the end for which he was created. He desires and needs to know the objective world; but he himself, his whence, his whither, his busi-

ness here, are more important to him. Moreover, as we have seen, the
human spirit is the interpreter of nature and science itself is impossible
except in so far as matter is brought under thought. The methods of science
are the bequest of the thinker; it is the image of God in man which gives
him the key to the material universe; only as he is awakened to self-know-
ledge can he truly know other things. The adoption of fruitful methods of
inquiry is vastly more important to science than the discovery of new facts.
Facts in themselves are nothing; they become significant only in their relation to principles; and the chief endeavor of science to-day is the improvement of its methods and the perfecting of its classification, for which it is
dependent on applied logic and intellectual insight.

The physical sciences, it will thus be seen, are not, in some important
respects, co-ordinate branches of general education; they are not entitled to
an equal rank with metaphysics, mathematics, philology and the mental
sciences. The latter are strictly first studies, furnishing the principles and
the instruments for all others. What then can the natural sciences do? They
are commended as practical studies; but practical in the sense of ministering
to the material wants of mankind belongs not to our subject. What can
they do in education? *First*, these sciences, occupied with the external world,
give elementary training to the perceptive faculties and engage all the senses
in the investigation of the facts of nature; thus delivering the soul from the
bondage of visionary abstractions and the dreams of idealism. *Secondly*,
they are particularly adapted to the improvement of a certain class of minds,
and thus become the instruments of intellectual awakening to some who
would never otherwise have known their capabilities; and they are also to
most minds an agreeable relief from the profounder attention required by
mathematics and philosophy, and give a change and a new spring to the
jaded mental powers. *Thirdly*, they connect the observation of facts with
the laws of thought, and in the hands of a skillful instructor may become
instruments of the most exact logical method and of the widest philosophical
generalization; and in this application they must be allowed to be of the
greatest value as a means of intellectual discipline. *Fourthly*, science and
metaphysics mutually supplement each other. The world of thought and
the world of matter are in correspondence; and the student of nature is
enabled often to make real and clear, to give actualization to the reflections
of the philosopher. Science seeks *the how* of things, philosophy *the why;*
but there is some point where these must meet and agree; the *a priori*
method will come down with its empty form of thought, the *a posteriori* will
carry up the material which is to fill and realize the form; and thus the great
circle of knowledge will be made complete. *Fifthly*, the relations of the
sciences have brought them into special prominence. Scientific reflection
has been pushed to the border-land of metaphysics and theology, and is
weeping to cross over and conquer these worlds. Science lies at the basis of
almost every living question between mere materialism and the Christian
faith. Its progress will undoubtedly affect the traditional interpretation of
portions of the Holy Scriptures; natural theology, also, though it will in the
end be placed upon a firmer basis, will need to be somewhat re-cast. The
Christian educator can not be silent on these questions in the class-room, the
minister in the pulpit can not altogether ignore them; and neither can afford
to have but a superficial acquaintance with them.

We now pass to the second division of our subject — the position to be
assigned to scientific studies in the college system of education. Do the
tendencies of the times indicate that the elementary education of youth in

this country is likely to be more special in its nature — practical, as it is called — or to be more universal, so that, so far as it goes, it shall fit the student for all spheres of activity? It is probable that other schools for special purposes will be multiplied; but will the college hold fast its profession of liberal training in the arts and sciences, or will it be modified by the special schools and become more like them? That it will remain substantially the same as it is now we have no doubt. The education which the college is to furnish must be of such a nature that it will not decide beforehand for the student what his course of life must be, but will rather give him the key to his capabilities, and enable him to choose freely his own vocation and decide his own destiny. It is precisely this grand purpose of education which the special and so-called practical schools never can accomplish, and hence they are really less practical than the liberal system.

If, now, this is the primary object of the college, to open the gates of knowledge in all directions and prepare the student for all spheres of life, what changes, if any, in the present course of studies is required, and, in particular, how large a place must be given to the natural sciences? As to the so-called demands of the times and the spirit of the age, to which many confidently appeal for the settlement of this question, we dismiss them from consideration, for the reason that the times and the age are an exceedingly doubtful and variable standard, and the methods of education must not be submitted to the popular vote, but determined by the widest and soundest principles. Let education be for the higher ideas, the higher faculties, and the higher modes of thought, or give up all things that are high! The question then is — What are the comparative values in a system of education, in their relation to the unfolding, the reforming, and the training of the mind; of scientific, linguistic, mathematical, and philosophical studies? To give the mind development and a right direction is more than to store it with facts; hence every study in any scheme of education must be pursued in a strictly scientific manner — that is, with reference to principles and system, rather than details.

What, now, is the power of language-study in education? This will properly include in it the departments of rhetoric and literature, so far as these are conducted on the basis of language-study. The formation of language exhibits the stages by which pure intellect becomes object to itself. In words the secret processes of thought are exposed; hence it is the most potent discipline of the whole course. The profound analysis and superior grasp of thought which this study gives have long been noted by educators. It is emphatically a culture-study. As a preparation also for the whole circle of metaphysical studies, its value is unequaled; hence the study of language must always form the principal basis of a college education. But why not study the modern languages, as German and French, instead of the so-called dead languages? We have no space for argument, and can only meagerly suggest. If the chief purpose of education is the development, discipline, and elevation of the mental powers, then the question whether we shall employ the ancient or the modern languages is not pertinent. What languages are best for that result? We hold that no modern languages are equal to the Latin and Greek as culture-studies. They belonged to the flowering period of human thought. The Greek is the classic for all time. As an instrument of education, let its scientific structure, its marvelous creations and its æsthetic influence on mind and heart, bear witness. So long as it can boast a Homer, a Plato, and a Gospel, more need not be urged against its exclusion from any course worthy of the term liberal. If the modern college can dispense with all that, in the interest of mere material investigation, then must the tendencies of modern life be simply to the surface and to the outside of things, or the modern college is doomed to short life.

As to the Latin, most of the tongues of modern Europe are only modifications of Latin, and can best be learned through Latin. Even our own English can better be approached from some of its sides through the same medium. Greek and Latin strike their roots into the very heart of English. From them we draw our terms for exact science, law, theology and medicine. If it be true that whoever speaks to the popular heart, draws his vocabulary from the old Anglo-Saxon bed, it is equally as true that whoever gives expression to high thought and reflection, resorts to Latin root-words. Grammar can not be learned from English, which has to so great an extent laid aside grammatical forms. It is to be remembered, moreover, that the study of Greek and Latin is the study of ancient history, of rhetoric and literature, in a word, is the study of humanity. But we must forbear. When one was asked what he got from all his Greek and Latin at Eton, he replied, "The power to get whatever else I like." The average classical scholar will, in a short time, overtake and pass the average specialist even in his own department. There need be no fear that the ancient classics will be unable to hold their place in the best colleges of this country.

The mathematics must be taught in college. As an instrument of education the mathematics, by almost universal consent, hold an important place. They involve attention and abstraction, the two processes which lie at the basis of all intellectual cultivation. They also set before us the most perfect type of deductive reasoning. We do not think, however, that exclusive attention to mathematics exerts so favorable an intellectual influence as the exclusive study of language and philosophy. The sphere of mathematics is the hard, dry forces of the intellect, not the organized system of human society and the powers of the human soul, not the humanities, not man in his completeness. And yet the college can not well dispense with any portion of the usual mathematical course. It can not, at least, well stop short of the calculus, which, as conducting the mind on from definite quantity to indefinite process, forms the proper transition from the material to the mental; and it should also include applied mathematics so far as to natural philosophy and astronomy, as examples of the application of the exact method to facts of observation.

The various mental sciences, such as logic, psychology, morals, philosophy, etc., constitute a necessary part of every liberal education. They lead to thoughtfulness and the awakening of the free activity of the mind. By means of these the individual passes out from the partial to the universal, from dependence to internal freedom and self-possession, which alone give true insight and practicalness to the intelligence. These studies, when sufficiently long pursued, are not only a training but a regeneration of the mind. Huxley, indeed, in his "Lecture on a Piece of Chalk" affirms that "the man who shall know the true history of a bit of chalk, if he will think his knowledge out to its ultimate results, is likely to have a truer and, therefore, a better conception of this wonderful universe and of man's relation to it, than the most learned student, who is deep read in the records of humanity and ignorant of those of nature." But we still think that the lecturer himself was a vastly more interesting subject of study than the piece of chalk he held in his hand, or, indeed than the whole cretaceous period; and we think there are depths in humanity profounder than physical science has line to measure. It is these introspective studies which give a peculiar balance to the faculties, which elevate the sentiments of men and enable them to know themselves. They correct the tendencies of the world, and, leading man into the interior sanctuary of his own nature, prevent a one-sided development in the direction of materialism and utilitarianism. We do not see how that education is complete for its purposes which assigns to these subjects an inferior place.

Must the present course, then, remain unchanged? There are some who say, " Yes; let the college go on as heretofore. Let those who want the new studies go to the special schools for them. The college as it has been has justified its right to be the college of the future." But this, we think is an extreme. If college education is to be in the high sense a generous education, it must embrace, so far as possible, the whole system of co-ordinated knowledge. The development of the physical sciences in our day, and the extension of intellectual interchange among nations, render necessary a widening of the circle of studies, in order to completeness in the system. Hence the physical sciences and the modern languages are entitled to a larger place than has hitherto been given them in the course. Others say, "Let us have optional studies. After a certain stage, the sophomore year perhaps, let the course be elective and let the student choose for himself what studies he will pursue, according to the bias of his genius and the purpose of his life, without prejudice to his degree." Now, one obvious difficulty in the way of the elective system is that only the largest colleges can successfully carry it out. The number of teachers must be correspondingly increased or the quality of the teaching must more than correspond-ingly deteriorate. It would be the extremest folly for nine-tenths of the colleges of this country, with their present teaching force, to attempt it. But further : the principle should first be settled. If the views which have now been advanced in this paper as to the requisites of a complete collegiate education are correct, or approximate correctness, the elective system is an inferior system, a concession to loose, popular demand, at the expense of sound scholarship and a full and symmetrical development of mind. That it has some advantages no one will deny. It is well for the student to be familar with microscopy, but is that an educational equivalent for Demosthenes or for Logic? The elective system is, in fact, just at the point where it begins, the termination of a liberal education and a divergence into professional schools; in other words, the attempt to found a university proper on the basis of the education of a sophomore. Now, we hold that the student should first acquire the power of mastering special subjects, and that this power is not to be gained by any limited and special employment of his faculties, which can be equally and evenly developed only by general cultivation and discipline. Nor must it be overlooked that in the elective system the danger is great, lest, in the multitude of studies set before him, the exact nature of which he may know but little about, the student be hurried from one thing to another, and do nothing well. If our institutions generally are compelled by high example to become schools, in great part, of mere practical or special education, let it be with the distinct understanding that it will be quite as certain to result in the degradation as in the popularization of the college system.

But without displacing the old studies, without relinquishing the old means and methods, the object sought of enlarging the old course so as to include the new studies, may perhaps be accomplished in another way : - First, the text-books and methods of teaching may be improved. Instead of making every study complete in itself, let it be completed only in its relation to the general system of studies. While the first principles and general applications of every subject are taught more thoroughly than ever before, let every excess of details, which only cumber the mind, be avoided. Secondly, the preparatory course may be extended. Three years of preparation are short enough for entrance into the Freshman class; but in these three years some of the Freshman studies of the present course would be included. This would make room for new studies in the upper classes, and is probably the practical solution of the problem of modern education to which we are coming. This is, at any rate, a solution in the right direction.

The cause of education is next in importance to the cause of religion, and must not be imperilled by unwise experiments. The American college is peculiar. It is the central idea in our whole system of education. It may not be already perfect; it does not profess to do everything; it is neither a professional school nor a university; but the American college has made the education of our people what it is, and still stands in the van of progress. *Esto perpetua*, with its grand ideal, *the place of Hard Work, Severe Discipline and High Culture!*

The discussion on this paper was opened by President DODGE, of Madison University. He was in favor of making our colleges and universities as complete and efficient as possible, and held that the capability of interpreting the ancient languages was of immense aid to ministers. They could, with this aid, go to the root of the Scriptures they taught; otherwise they would be compelled to accept knowledge at second hand. There would be no fear of science or of speculative learning, if the foundations are secure. Collegiate education should be prized, not alone for its practical use, as is too much the inclination now-a-days, but for the culture and breadth of view which it gives.

Dr. MOSS, of Philadelphia, regarded the paper as one of high order. He protested against so much stress being laid upon the so-called practical education of the day. It is coming to be considered too much of a mere instrumentality for making money. Education is becoming too materialized. It was not well to run all to utility, leaving out the higher aims and objects of intellectual culture. There should be a wise blending of both. No system of thought could offer higher or truer culture than that promoted by the religion of Christ. Christian educators should never allow themselves to separate religion and mental culture. Combined, they produced the highest condition of man.

Prof. CLARKE, of Ohio, advocated collegiate education, as conferring the highest benefits upon the student. Without it, full intellectual discipline is impossible. It is of the highest value, even when not immediately applicable to the every-day concerns of life.

Hon. MARK H. DUNNELL, of Minnesota, advocated the necessity and usefulness of high schools as feeders of the colleges. He thought them the best thing that could be had in the newly-settled portions of the West, where denominational academies are impossible. The classics should be introduced into them as a part of the regular course of studies. This arrangement would add greatly to their value, and at the same time constitute them more largely the supporters of our colleges.

President ANDERSON, of Rochester University, expressed his gratification at the interest manifested in collegiate education. He regarded it as a most favorable indication, and its general prevalence indicated that great progress had been made in this direction. He had been deeply interested in the discussions to which he had listened, as well as in the papers read.

The PRESIDENT spoke briefly touching the progress of the educational interests of the Baptists. They had made such progress that they would not suffer in a comparison with those of any other denomination. The great want is a more liberal support of our higher educational institutions. But we are gradually improving in this respect, and will continue to improve as the question is discussed and becomes better understood.

The President of the Convention announced that he should be compelled to leave the city, and would therefore resign his position as presiding officer. He expressed his gratification at the evidences of interest in education which this Convention afforded, and his thanks for the courtesy extended to himself.

His resignation was accepted, and the Hon. MARK H. DUNNELL, LL.D., of Minnesota, was elected President in his stead.

The Convention then adjourned, with prayer by Rev. E. E. L. TAYLOR, D.D., of New York.

EVENING SESSION.

The Convention was called to order by the President at half-past seven o'clock P.M. Prayer was offered by Rev. F. A. DOUGLASS, of Ohio.

On motion of Dr. CUTTING it was voted to publish the minutes and the papers read in Convention; and a committee consisting of Rev. D. H. COOLEY, of Illinois, Prof. A. N. CURRIER, of Iowa, and Rev. F. A. DOUGLASS, of Ohio, was appointed to raise funds for the purpose.

After singing a hymn, the Convention listened to a paper by Rev.
J. A. SMITH, D.D., of Illinois, upon

THE COLLEGES AND UNIVERSITIES OF THE WEST.

The subject assigned for this paper is, *The Colleges and Universities of
the West, their Present Character and Functions, with the Possible Lines
of their Development to meet the Advancing Needs of Education.*

Of inst'tutions bearing the name of " College," or " University," within
the territory contemplated here, and connected with the Baptist denomination, there are eleven, viz.: Kalamazoo College, at Kalamazoo, Mich.;
Denison University, at Granville, Ohio; Franklin College, at Franklin,
Ind.; Shurtleff College, at Upper Alton, Ill.; William Jewell College, at
Liberty, Mo.; Ottawa University, at Ottawa, Kansas; Burlington College,
at Burlington, Iowa; DesMoines University, at DesMoines, Iowa; Central
University, at Pella, Iowa; Wayland University, at Beaver Dam, Wis.; and
the University of Chicago. It is proper to add that at Hastings, Minn., an
institution was founded by the Baptist State Convention, some years ago,
under the style of a University. Unexpected difficulties were met in the
development of the undertaking, and it was finally decided to defer, for
the present, the establishment of a school of that grade. There is, however,
now a corporation, bearing the title of " The Minnesota Central University,"
to which, upon the abandonment of the enterprise at Hastings, the fund up
to that time secured for this purpose, with the attendant responsibilities, was
passed over. The fund alluded to now amounts to some $6,000 or $8,000,
and is to continue invested while the undertaking remains in suspense, and
the developments of the future are awaited. In the meantime, a school of
the higher academical grade is conducted at Waseoga, by Rev. L. B. Allen,
D.D. The grounds belonging to this school, ten acres in extent, were
secured several years since by the Freewill Baptists, and a commodious stone
building erected. By the failure of their plans the property reverted to the
town, and the town authorities tendering it to the Baptists upon the condition of maintaining there an Academy, the offer was accepted. Under Dr.
Allen's charge a prosperous school is in progress, with classical, literary and
scientific departments. There is also a partial course in theology, for the
benefit of such brethren contemplating the ministry as are unable to seek a
more extended one elsewhere.

It should also be mentioned that the Baptist State Convention of Wisconsin, in view of the obstacles to a present or speedy consummation of the
plan for building up a university at Beaver Dam, has entered into an arrangement with the University of Chicago, by which Wayland University is put
in connection with the Preparatory Department of that institution. Meanwhile, in Wisconsin as in Minnesota, the enterprise of founding a school of
the university or college grade, though not abandoned, remains in abeyance,
awaiting what the future may bring.

Of those schools upon our list which have already reached the college
grade there are six: Kalamazoo College, Denison University, Shurtleff
College, Franklin College, William Jewell College, and the University of
Chicago. The name " University," adopted by the others, indicates rather
what is aimed at, for the future, than what is claimed in the present. One
of them, the Ottawa University, in Kansas, is certainly warranted by its
large endowments in land in anticipating a time not distant, when its
faculty of instruction and its course of study may realize a development well

toward the measure of the original design. At all of them excellent educational work is done, and both those now in care of them whether as teachers or as trustees, as well as those into whose labors these have entered, should be mentioned with all honor as sharing nobly in the work of promoting the intellectual and moral culture of the Great West.

It will be noticed that in the enumeration made, three institutions, with the title of "University" or "College" are located in Iowa. Of these, the one at DesMoines is most recent in date. It has already had experience of the difficulties of a new enterprise, yet as a school enjoys an excellent reputation. It receives both ladies and gentlemen; numbering, at the present time, fifty-one in the former department, thirty-five in the latter; eighty-six in all. Its property is valued at $45,000.

Central University, at Pella, was opened in 1854. Students in it are conducted in classical study as far as to the Freshman or Sophomore class in college, and are then advised to go elsewhere to complete their course, a large proportion of them entering the State University at Iowa City. There is a more extended scientific course for such as desire it. This school also includes both ladies and gentlemen, of whom an aggregate of twenty-three hundred have been in attendance from the beginning; the aggregate for the current year being one hundred and ninety-four. The property, in buildings, grounds, library, etc., is estimated at $25,000, besides which a sum of $10,000, as the beginning of an endowment, has recently been secured. Young men study in that school preparatory to the ministry, to the law, and for the profession of teachers.

Burlington College, located at Burlington, may be classed among the earlier educational undertakings in the West. The hope of its founders has always been that it would in due time become in fact what it is in name, and its course of study, arranged in six schools, manifestly provides for this. Its property, in building and grounds attractive in site and of good dimensions, amounts to some $30,000. It has an invested fund of $17,000, bearing interest at from seven to ten per cent., and a library and apparatus — the former containing two thousand volumes — which are valued at $4,000. It has thus, either in real estate, in interest-bearing funds, or in other valuable assets, a property of $50,000, entirely unincumbered. The whole number in attendance, during the year ending June 21st, has been sixty-eight, of whom thirty-eight were females and five theological students. The range of study embraces a considerable amount of what is taught in colleges. In the estimation of intelligent friends of education in Iowa — though others equally entitled to respect hold different views — it is the preferable course to maintain this institution at Burlington, as well as those at Pella and at DesMoines for the present, simply as first-class collegiate schools. leaving the question of a fully-endowed college and its location to be determined hereafter.

Those of our institutions which at present hold the college grade have had full experience of the vicissitudes incident to the history of educational enterprises in a country wholly or comparatively new. Franklin College, after a considerable period of useful service, under the presidency, first of Dr. Chandler, afterwards of Dr. Silas Bailey, was for a few years suspended, and grave doubts have been felt by its friends as to the possibility of replacing it in a career of hopeful progress. Self-denying and enterprising brethren, however, took up the work where financial difficulties, variously caused, had compelled others to lay it down; and now, under the presidency of Dr. H. L. Wayland, it is resuming its place among the colleges of the land. The effort to raise a professorship endowment of $100,000 is advancing prosperously, while a full college faculty and a complement of college classes will no doubt be soon announced. William Jewell College suffered heavily from the late war, and was indeed for a time entirely suspended, with little apparent prospect of recovery from its disasters. Three years since an effort to revive it was entered upon, and has been signally successful. The college now has property, in buildings and grounds, valued at $40,000, and a professorship endowment of $100,000. Under the administration of Dr. Thomas Rambaut, the President, with his associates in a faculty of five professors besides himself, it has achieved a measure of public favor that warrants the expectation of soon completing its endowment and providing it with all the equipments of a first-class college. Others, like Shurtleff and Kalamazoo, while less endangered in their existence by such vicissitudes, have had full experience of the ordeals so occasioned, although now, it is believed, in a position to feel less seriously the effect of changes and reverses.

In speaking of the place filled by our Western colleges among institutions of this class throughout the land, we would not wish to claim more than is fairly their due, yet, upon the other hand, must not be expected to undervalue them. They are a part of our Western growth, and partake of those characteristics which the West as a whole necessarily bears. What they have gained in endowments, in lands and buildings, in public favor, in literary standing, they have so gained as the fruit of strenuous exertion. They have received from the State simply the charters that make them legal corporations. Their beginnings have often been small, and their progress has been in a road beset with difficulties. Vicissitudes and reverses have been inevitable. Large subscriptions have more than once been lost in consequence of general financial derangement putting it out of the power of those making them to fulfill their pledges. A period of lively hope has been often closely followed by a period of discouragement and depression, when faith, patience and persistence have been taxed to the utmost. Debt and the consequent embarrassment have been found more or less unavoidable, while the resources of energy and hopefulness in those upon whom the care and the work devolved have been in some instances well-nigh consumed in contending with the enormous difficulties so caused. If any of these college enterprises have been premature, or in any other way at fault in their inception, that was purely an error of judgment under circumstances rendering it eminently excusable, and on the part of men whose public spirit, and energy, and self-devotion might cover and extenuate far more serious mistakes.

That, in these circumstances, Western colleges have succeeded thus early in achieving their present measure of financial strength and literary power, is certainly much to their credit. The oldest of them has not seen forty years of history, while the majority of them are not yet a quarter of a century old. The period within which they have claimed full rank as colleges is even less. It is simply just that they be judged in the light of all these facts. At the same time it is not necessary to speak of even these things in any way of apology. The scholarship of Western colleges may not have all the breadth of that found in some Eastern ones, yet in the essentials of a classical, scientific and literary training it is believed to be no less thorough and complete. They have upon their faculties scholars and instructors whose reputation is national; while, if others have not yet achieved this position, it may be said of them that they are meriting it, both by their talents, their personal culture, and the fidelity and efficiency with which their daily work is done. Western students, besides, in seeking the advantages of a collegiate training, do so, for the most part, with the earnest purpose characteristic of the Western mind. A young man here enters upon life, as a rule, thoroughly comprehending that he has his career not only to choose, but to make. He comes to the college, often, imperfectly prepared for the higher grades of study, but with "a mind to work," so that the disadvantage of this defective preparation is in most instances successfully surmounted by subsequent zealous and resolute application. Such opportunities as offer, in the mutual relations of colleges, to judge of comparative attainment, would indicate that the Western student ranks fairly with the Eastern one. Young men from our colleges going to Eastern colleges find no difficulty in entering there with the same grade as here, while instances have occurred of students failing to maintain standing in a Western college and being received to an advanced standing in an Eastern one. Such facts are only mentioned as showing that so far as these interchanges represent the standard of scholarship and the measure of attainment in Eastern and Western colleges, respectively, the practical result is at least not to our discredit; and as showing, also, that in the essentials of a collegiate course the Western college — young, and in some respects immature, as it may be — may justly, in comparison with the Eastern one, assert its right to the honorable designation it bears.

Such defects as appear in the courses of study so far adopted in the colleges of the West are chiefly due, it would seem, to two causes : the necessity of having respect in them to the imperfect preparation of the student upon entering, and deficient provision of instruction occasioned by deficiency of endowments. The preparatory departments connected with the several colleges enable them to control the first of these conditions in some degree, and this, with the perfecting of our academical system, generally, will no doubt in time so far surmount the difficulty as to bring the student to his college course with a measure of scholarship preparing him to encounter on more equal terms the ordeals of advanced study. It needs no argument in detail to show how much more breadth, variety, and completeness a scholar's work may have, where he enters upon it with a mastery of first principles such as both warrants and facilitates scholarly enterprise. A more ample provision of instructors, however, would even then be necessary : such as that the several professors, no longer overworked as they now are in class-drill, may have both leisure and strength for that more discursive and suggestive method of teaching which the lecture supplies ; such also as may render practicable opportunities for special study when such are desired. To this more ample endowments are plainly indispensable.

It is simply claimed for our Western collegiate course as it now stands that it embraces, in the classics, in modern languages, in mathematics, pure and applied, in science, in philosophy and in letters, what in any American college is considered in the strict sense essential. In arranging it, the American system is adopted, with modifications in certain particulars. Thus the separate scientific course is more common in Western colleges than in Eastern ones, especially those of the same grade. Hence, the eclectic principle is probably with us allowed freer scope. William Jewell College divides its course of study into schools, such as the School of Greek, the School of Latin, the School of Mathematics, the School of Natural Sciences, the School of English and History, the School of Theology, and others. Students are received in these several schools "upon probation," and only matriculated as members of the college after fair trial of their scholarship. They may graduate from one or more of the schools after due examination. Each school, for the completion of its assigned course, seems to require three

years of study, styled, the Junior, the Intermediate, and the Senior   For
students who need more elementary instruction in any one of them, there is
also a Sub-Junior Class. The courses adopted in our other colleges vary
from the customary one only in certain special features. Thus, in the University of Chicago and in Franklin College a different order from the usual
one is preferred in the studies belonging to the department of Philosophy.
Metaphysics is assigned for the Junior year. Logic and Moral Philosophy for
the Senior; the reason being that an acquaintance with the principles of
Metaphysics seems essential to the most successful prosecution of studies,
like Logic and Moral Philosophy, into which they so largely enter. In the
Western college classical study is made to occupy its long-established place
in the American as well as the European curriculum. It is to be hoped that
such will continue to be the fact, and that one feature of that development
and enlargement which is expected as resources increase, will be a measure
of culture in this department commensurate with that afforded in each other
one. Even should our Western scholarship, in accordance with tendencies
of the Western mode of thought, come to rate ever so highly the practical and
the available, it will not, it is believed, any the less value what is so essential
in a generous culture while it opens doors to ranges of literature so rich and
wide.

Leaving now, however, these details, the object of which has been to afford
something like an adequate view of the character and condition of Western
Baptist colleges, the remainder of this paper will be devoted to the consideration of two or three general questions having reference more to what may be
anticipated in the future of these institutions.

1. First of all, it is believed to be a condition fundamental to that larger
development for which we hope, and that better adjustment of our whole
denominational system of higher education in the West, that our brethren
generally shall come to rate more adequately the functions of the college, and
the collegiate course of study, considered simply in itself.

It was unquestionably an admirable thing in those who were early upon
the ground in these newer States, that they saw so clearly, and felt so profoundly, the great claim of the opening field around them, as a field to be
cultivated in the interests of truth; and that they were so prompt and so
much in earnest in asking, "Whence are to come the sowers and the reapers
in the vast spiritual husbandry of the West?"   It was natural, and it was
right, for them to feel that among the earliest and most urgent wants of this
region would be the school for the education of ministers. Pressed by that
conviction, they began to make provision to this end as almost the first purpose of denominational enterprise and union. Hence it has resulted that in
founding colleges, or institutions out of which it was proposed to make colleges, in time, the main thought has been, "It is for the education of our
Western Baptist ministry." Brethren charged with the practical care and
work of such enterprises, have felt this so strongly in themselves, and have
seen its influence so much among the churches, that naturally, and quite
properly, they have put it forward as the grand plea in behalf of such interests. Entirely becoming as this was, it is a question whether there has not
resulted from it a predisposition, on the part of many of the best friends of
our colleges and universities, to value them almost solely in proportion as
they are schools for educating ministers. Surely the time has now come, at
least, when we may, in our sympathies and plans, embrace other interests
with this, and may remind ourselves of what a good college essentially is,
apart from any one of its more especial designs.

It is a very important and hopeful feature of the American collegiate system that it is to such an extent framed and directed by religious men, and controlled by the various religious denominations. All experience shows that education purely secular tends to skepticism and ungodliness, while nothing is more needed, even in the highest ranges of study and inquiry, than that reverence for revealed truth which may save men from the misleading tendencies of intellectual vanity. To separate learning from religion is to make it the plaything of human caprice, or the instrument of human irreligiousness; while science itself, though ever so wide in its research and rich in its results, is left at the mercy of mere speculation until it may scarcely have enough of either clear discernment or steady faith to know even the man from the brute. Besides, it is plainly right that all of human culture, as all of human achievement in other respects, religion shall conse-crate. The Christian people of a country like ours, should not suppose that their work, as such, begins and ends with the establishment of churches and the provision of a ministry. They are in circumstances to influence in favor of what is true, and pure, and honoring to God, the whole national develop-ment; and in no respect more than in that of the national culture. Here the college finds its sphere. Planted by a denomination of Christian people, its chairs filled by men who love Christian truth and know how discreetly to mingle its inculcation with that of true knowledge in other things, embracing in its course of study the Christian evidences and the moral principles fun-damental to all right faith and right life, honoring God in daily worship and daily reading of the Scriptures, while the Christian example and testimony of pious teachers and pious students appeal unanswerably to conviction and to every best feeling,—such an institution, above and beyond all that it is in an intellectual point of view, is a power for good, religiously, whose effect enters into the hearts and lives of those who make our national history, moulds those whose work it will ever after be to mould others, and perpetu-ates itself, and widens, with the generations and the ages.

Then it is a privilege by no means to be undervalued, that of sharing in the work of higher education. Baptists, apart from what is due to them-selves as a religious denomination, and apart from all consideration of the value to them as a people of the sympathy and good will of such, educated in their schools, as may ever after retain a sense of personal indebtedness and a consequent kindly interest, though unconnected with them denominationally — apart from all that, Baptists should rate highly the opportunity they have, and the power they have, to bear their part fully in the general service of national culture. Our colleges should be valued just in that view of their functions. They should be made as ample in their resources as possible, as complete in all their equipments, as efficient in every element of literary power, in order that we may take our place squarely beside the best and foremost in this work, and may be able, not with pride, but with just self-appreciation to declare that we are " not a whit behind the very chiefest." To this it is plainly essential that our generous brethren adequately appreciate the function of the college in this point of view, and realize how worthy an object it is for their most liberal donations, to thus render our denominational college system, simply as such, equal to the best in the land.

The practical bearing of this view, in one respect, may be seen if we notice a class of facts connected with national legislation. Some writer has been at the pains to ascertain how many members of the present Con-gress are college graduates, and where they were educated. He finds that "of 265 members, 99 have had an education in institutions known as colleges and universities, 71 are recorded as educated in academies, and the remaining 95 as educated at home or in the public schools. The ninety-nine college graduates were educated in fifty-five different colleges in this country and one in Europe. No college sends more than Yale, which numbers six. Next comes Western Reserve college and Brown University, with five each, and these are followed by Princeton and Union with four each." Harvard College has only three. This writer calls special attention to the fact that a Western college ranks next to Yale in the number it sends to the present Congress. Of the whole number, 99, of college graduates now in Congress, he notes the fact that only twenty are from New England, and adds: "The nation's destiny has already passed to new hands, and the influence of our old colleges and universities, as well as of Eastern usages and habits of thought, has relatively declined. Western Reserve College, with its five graduates in Congress, takes precedence of the oldest college in New England, which has but three!" * * "The nation's destiny," he says, "in the hands of its representatives is to be determined by the character of the population that is so rapidly filling the Mississippi Valley. Whether they shall have educated men to represent it in Congress, and whether these educated men shall be trained under Christian influence, is one of the most important questions which it falls to the living generation to determine." This testimony of an intelligent Eastern man may be emphatically commended to the consideration of the men of the West.

2. Another point proposed for consideration here relates to the multiplication of colleges.

The territorial lines fixed in the political organization of this country very naturally, and to a certain extent properly, influence organization in other respects. It is found both convenient and serviceable to arrange missionary work, and other joint enterprises in accordance with outlines thus ready-made and suggestive. It is clearly possible, however, for these territorial lines to create distinctions where there is really no difference, and to interfere with that sort of union for which such lines should have no existence whatever. There can be no good reason, for example, why the interest of higher education, even as represented in particular institutions, should not be an interest common to all the States; no good reason why it should be thought a disparagement to one State that its young men receive such education in some other State; no good reason why to give money for the endowment of colleges in another State than one's own should be viewed as giving support to something foreign or competitory; no good reason why interests which *are* comparatively local should be crippled by premature attempts to localize this one which is in such a large sense common to all. These points, it is believed safe to assume in this argument; and there will then remain simply the question what principle ought to govern in the founding of new institutions of the higher grade, and to decide, in general, as to the number and location of Baptist colleges in the West.

It is respectfully submitted whether such a principle may not be stated thus: That colleges should *now and hereafter* be created with a view to meet, not *anticipated*, but *actual* needs of the denomination; and so far as present resources may warrant, not with a lien upon resources of the future.

A time comes, in the development of any new country, when such a practical rule as this becomes sound and safe. Upon foundations early laid, structures have risen adequate to meet existing needs, and that necessity once so stringent of anticipating both wants and resources ceases to be felt. It is a fair question whether that time has not now come for us in the West. If an exception be allowed, it must be in behalf of that farther West for which the Ottawa University in Kansas seems intended to provide. Even as respects those remoter districts it must be conceded that the existing pressure is not so urgent as to make it imperative upon us to embarrass other work in order to push this one to a speedier result. With existing facilities of travel, the Western student, though his home should be in the very shadow of the Rocky Mountains, may make his choice among half-a-dozen colleges, more or less accessible to him. Without doubt, the movement to secure a basis of ultimate large endowment, such as we now have at Ottawa, was wise; but it is believed that without serious detriment even that institution may, for its more complete organization, await the sure and steady growth of the noble State in the heart of which it is planted; and its friends not fear that they are losing valuable time if the work of endowment proves to be slower than they had hoped.

There are strong reasons to be urged for each of the opposite views held upon the subject of the multiplication of colleges — a subject of such great practical interest to us in the West. Upon the one hand, it is not to be denied that even a very few fully-endowed and efficient colleges accomplish a better present work than many such, all poor, all embarrassed, and each necessarily crippled in its work by its poverty in educational means If the question were now a new one, and if we had at this moment to decide how many colleges our denomination in the West shall undertake to found and sustain, those who would severely limit the number might have arguments to urge which it would be difficult to answer. But, upon the other hand, the question is not a new one. To a certain extent it must be conceded that the point as to the number of our colleges is one already settled. Each of those whose names have been given as having reached the college grade has made for itself a position, a history, a hold upon public confidence and denominational sympathy such as that probably no one amongst us would go so far as to say that either should be denied the right to live. Then, it must be conceded that colleges, while they subserve various other denominational and general interests, supply stimulus, also, to educational zeal, and while prosecuting their assigned and expected work educate the denomination itself to a higher view and purpose in this regard. Some, impressed by these and other considerations, would say that schools of this class ought to be increased to that extent, at least, that each State may have its own college. The correctness of this view may be admitted, if we look simply to the remote future, and speak of the time when all these Western States shall be full of people and full of wealth, and when to endow a college shall no longer be, as it is now, the work of a generation. Speaking with reference to things as they are, the suggestion is ventured whether what we have already begun should not, at least, be put in a position of safety from financial shipwreck before more is attempted. Besides, time may thus be afforded for the quiet adjustment, through the logic of events, of local questions which may now be difficult to manage. If the friends of institutions whose plan, as yet unconsummated, contemplates a college or university organization, will consent for the time to aim simply at what is now practicable, and leave all questions of a State college or its location to the future, availing themselves for the purposes of higher education of the colleges we already have, much may be gained in point of denominational union, simplicity of plan, and means to complete present beginnings. For the present, the idea of a college for every State in the West is not even a practical one. The brethren in Wisconsin and Minnesota are. It is believed, wise in allowing this question to remain simply in its theoretical shape, and consenting to wait until resources shall be larger and the need more pressing before attempting what is so apt to prove simply an embarrassment and a cause of division.

If the view thus taken is just, the conclusion would seem to be, that while the colleges we now actually have should be fostered, and as rapidly as possible put in a condition of the highest efficiency, other enterprises of this kind may most wisely be held in abeyance till our denominational means become more abundant, and our denominational want, in that respect, more urgent An important additional suggestion seems to be afforded by the character and position of those other institutions in our list which have the college or university name, although not properly occupying that grade. These, if less than colleges, are more than academies. Perhaps an appropriate designation for them may be that of collegiate schools. They not only conduct students into the first years of a college course, but they furnish instruction in theology, with the help of which some of our most efficient ministers in the West have prepared for their work. The place they fill, just as they are, is evidently an important one. Some of them must ultimately become colleges in fact. Meanwhile, if under the direction of such men as now conduct them, they may furnish a measure of educational training much to be valued, even if the circumstances of the student forbid its further prosecution, and render a most valuable service in the distinct province of ministerial education. They should, it is believed, as collegiate schools, be regarded as filling a place in our Western educational system peculiar and important.

3. One other special point demands attention : the place of the University in the collegiate system of our denomination for the West.

What the American university is ultimately to become, is a question as yet far from settled; although it is gratifying to know that in certain influential quarters it is beginning to receive the consideration it merits. We may, however, anticipate the result of such inquiry, so far as to say that the university method adopted in this country will doubtless be shaped in a large degree by the form of our school system in general, and by our national needs and characteristics. It is not likely, judging from present appearances, that we shall ever have universities, for example, made up of a group of colleges, like those of Oxford and Cambridge in England; the vast extent of our territory requiring that colleges shall be distributed, rather than concentrated. Nor is it likely that our university organization will ever, as in France, come to embrace the entire educational system, from the lowest schools up to the highest; the tendency with us being more in the direction of independent organization, with simply general mutual relations. Nor, as in Scotland, will it probably ever be true that, as a competent authority there has said, the university "is not an university only, but a high school, to supply the deficiency of other schools;" it being presumable that our "other schools" will not have deficiencies such as to demand a remedy so elaborate, but that the university will be needed, rather, to take up their work where they lay it down, and carry it on to completion. Neither is it likely that the German or the Italian system will be strictly reproduced in the American one. It must be a long time, indeed, before an American university can, like that of Heidelberg, in Germany, support sixty learned professors, each devoting himself to his own especial branch of knowledge; before, as in the German universities as a class, the number of students seeking such advanced instruction will either justify or sustain lecturers so numerous, and each so occupied with his own specialty, as that there shall remain scarcely a handbreadth of unexplored ground in all the world of learning

While, besides, as is evident even from what has now been said, the European universities do themselves so entirely fail to build after any one model, they can not fairly criticise our American one if it, also, adopts a model of its own and becomes what the country and the age require that it shall be. At the same time, we shall be fairly open to criticism if we do not at least seek to realize that one university ideal, which, originating with the universities of Bologna and Paris, in the Middle Ages, may be traced in Europe under all these diversities of form. This ideal evidently is, that a university shall not only be the flower and perfection of all the schools, but that it shall both attempt and accomplish what all the other schools combined necessarily fail in; and that is, a comprehension within its scheme of instruction, so far as possible, of the whole range of human learning, and, at the same time, the prosecution of inquiry in new directions, or of more thorough inquiry in old directions, and thus, at the same time, scrutinizing the known, and pushing on farther and farther into the regions of the knowable. It is plain, then, that our American university must be more than a college; more even than a college with its cluster of professional schools. It must be a place where learning will be sought for learning's own sake, and where shall be trained, not only American ministers, lawyers, doctors, engineers, agriculturists, but American scholars.

It seems at present most likely that the nucleus of the American university, wherever established, will be a college; such appears to be the tendency now, and to it there can be no objection. The university scheme, too, will probably embrace a system of professional schools / We shall, it may be presumed, so far disregard the dictum of Mr. John Stuart Mill, as to hold, in harmony with the practical character of the American genius, that the university *is*, for one of its functions at least, "a place of professional education." But this must not be all. Though its scheme in this respect should include all the professions, this alone will not make it a university. It must also put to practical use that distinction which an able English writer, Professor Seeley, makes between *education* and *learning;* must be a place where men shall not only be taught, but where they shall *teach themselves*, and, with the aid of the provision there furnished, go on beyond what the practical detail of any profession calls for, and ascend to the heights that are highest. Besides, it is fair to presume that for American scholars there may be departments of inquiry, either for the development of new truth, or the more accurate re-stating of old truth, specially reserved. What Germany does in Philology, France in Mathematics, England in Literature, Scotland and Germany, to some extent, in Philosophy, it may fall to America to do in some related sphere; perhaps in a clearer and safer expounding of philosophy itself; perhaps in departments of applied science; perhaps in that supremely important matter, the relation of science to religion. Has not this youngest and most vigorous of the nations a mission here? And is it not time for American scholars, and American friends of education, to realize that there is something more and greater in learning than education simply?

It may be that in the West a complete university will not be witnessed by the generation now living The question, however, which is here submitted, is, whether, in what we plan in this respect, we should not aim at that which ought to be, and which, according to all that we can now see, must be? Is it not competent for us to say, and is it not our duty to say, that we will mean by a university a university; something more than a college; more than a college with two or three professional schools attached? Ought we not to adjust our other institutions to this ideal, and say that our colleges shall be simply colleges, our collegiate schools shall be collegiate schools only, till they can be more; our academies academies, and that we will mean by a university strictly what the name imports? We, now living, may not see the ideal fully accomplished, but we shall have the satisfaction of working toward it, and those who come after us will not have occasion to say that our work has embarrassed theirs.

If so much as has now been said is accepted, it will follow that, for a long time to come, the denomination in the West will need to concentrate its interest and means to this end at some one point. If we are to have a university indeed, we can, in the very nature of the case, have *but* one. There must be, in buildings, in endowments, in libraries, in facilities of instruction, a provision which can be made adequate only as a result of concentration, and steady, patient, generous, wide-minded combination. As an incentive to this, it may be remembered that an institution such as we suppose, maintaining suitable relations to other institutions, would be a helper to all. It would aid them in elevating their standard of scholarship, supply stimulus both to their teachers and their students, be a center of intellectual power and interest for all alike, and, in gathering treasures of learning, constitute a source of supply ever more and more valuable. There is, in the mere hope of a confederacy in learning thus friendly and helpful, a prospect so noble that it might sufficiently reward us who are now living, to have simply been permitted to lay its corner-stone. Surely, since the West is beginning to lead in so many things, it may aspire to leadership also in this; and since, as Baptists, we so much have our educational mission still to fulfill, why may we not begin at this point to plan with a larger hope and a higher aim?

A point suggests itself here which, although not belonging strictly to the subject of this paper, is still in such an important relation with it that it should be at least touched in a few words. One university for the West implies one theological school, properly so called. For the systematic course in divinity plainly belongs with those other professional courses which are here supposed to be embraced in the scheme of the one university. The question will then, no doubt, occur to some, Will not, under such an arrangement, the aims and hopes of the founders of our colleges in this regard be disappointed, and what they had provided for the instruction of the Western Baptist ministry be turned exclusively to the interest of secular education? In answer to this, it may be said that the college itself, with reference to its college course purely is a school for ministerial education; that course being so material a preparation for the theological one, as that the latter without the former comparatively fails of its end. But then, further, it is submitted to the Boards of those colleges where this matter is felt to be of vital importance, whether a most important service in the distinct work of theological instruction — and all which can really be attempted without overburdening the resources of the college — may not be secured in the endowment of a theological professorship as a part of the regular college course. Such a course, with such an amount of study in various branches of theological study as should be included, and pursued from beginning to end with the understanding that it is the student's preparation for ministerial work, might send him forth fairly endowed for that work, while for many brethren it would be a measure and kind of preparation better suited to their circumstances than a more elaborate one. If it should be said that in one Western college this plan, upon trial, has been thought not consistent with the maintenance of a desirably high standard in the strictly college course, it may be also said, in reply, that in another it is now being prosecuted successfully. Should this expedient be found acceptable and practicable, it will take away one ground of difference in the views and plans of our educators in the West, and enable us to secure a desirable concentration of interest and means in the promotion of theological learning in its stricter and larger sense.

The result of all that has been said, then, seems to be this : that we nave in our Western Baptist colleges institutions fairly entitled to the name they bear, and which, in their present condition and literary standing invite not only the confidence of the denomination, but an energetic and generous co-operation in the work of completing their endowments and putting them every way in a condition of the highest efficiency; that in the schools founded with the design of making them colleges in due time, but not as yet arrived at that stage, we have a class of institutions, excellently adapted to the special service they now render, and justified in anticipating a development, in due time, most of them at least, to the rank of colleges in fact; that, however, it is better for these schools, filling as they do a place intermediate between the college and the academy, to remain as they are, even for an indefinite period, than by any forced effort to elevate them, or any one of them, at once to the college grade, to increase the number of partially endowed colleges, and embarrass and hinder the general interest of higher education; that it is now time for us to distinguish strictly between the university and the college, and that while accepting the theory that colleges must be multiplied as fast, though emphatically *no faster* than the demand requires, and the resources warrant, the very nature of the university organization requires that we shall have but one, so located as in the speediest and best way to be built up in the true proportions of a university, and embracing within its scheme along with other professional courses our *one* theological school; that at the same time the college course is susceptible of modification so as that the college also shall be for such as so desire a school of ministerial preparation, and thus our plan for such education, while it shall have more concentration in one direction, be made to have, at the same time, more scope and variety in another.

These views are submitted to the Convention, and to Baptist educators and friends of education in the West, with a diffident consciousness how very delicate as well as important are many of the questions involved, yet with a frankness which the duty assigned called for, and confidence in the indulgence and intelligence of the brethren has inspired.

NOTE.

In the enumeration of colleges and universities at the beginning of the above paper, one at least ought to have been included, La Grange College, at La Grange, in Missouri. This institution, embracing males and females, deserves to rank with the best of the collegiate schools, although not as yet ranking fully as a college. Its building occupies a handsome site, overlooking the Mississippi, while as a school, under the Presidency of Dr. Cook, it enjoys a large patronage and does excellent educational work. Elmira College, in Illinois, was regarded by the writer of this paper as belonging more properly to the institutions whose work is so well discussed by Dr.

Wayland; a remark which may also be made of Mount Carroll Seminary—
like the one just named, an excellent school. Another, fully ranking with
these, Rural Park Seminary, at Upper Alton, we regret to say, is announced
as suspended.

The CHAIR announced that the subject of the paper just read
was now open for discussion.

Dr. CUTTING wished to refer to a matter connected with the
general subject of the paper — that of the State institutions which
have been established in the West.   These institutions are facts, and
they will exist and abide in the land.   The question for us was our
relations to them.   He referred to the University of Michigan.   He
would not say that the Baptists of Michigan should not avail themselves of the advantages of this University.   But have they no other
duty in the cause of Christian education?   He thought they had.
It may not be advisable to attempt a university in Michigan, but a
college we should have.   If we rely upon high schools we shall fail
in securing recruits for our ministry.   It was not proposed to establish academies everywhere, but only in such places as they were
needed, and where they could be supported.   He referred to Phillips
Academy as an example of what an academy should be.

Prof. OLNEY, of Michigan, said that from beginning to end the
paper had his entire approbation.   He regarded its suggestions as
eminently wise ; and if they were carried out he thought we should
enter upon a new and upward career of progress.   He made some
remarks concerning academies.   It is not feeders that are so much
wanted as food at the places where students are to be.fed.   Give our
universities and colleges adequate endowments, and they would
exert an influence which would attract students.

Prof. TEN BROEK said that the foundation of the University
was actually laid as long ago as 1817, when Michigan contained but
six thousand people, half of whom could not read.   Although it
had a beginning and a charter so long ago, it was not an actual University until 1841.   This shows that the idea of beginning early with
our higher institutions is not a new thing.   The main point is, that
an early beginning has accomplished that which has been accomplished in Michigan, to which reference has been made.

Prof. ALLEN, of Minnesota, spoke in relation to the University
of that State, and to the institution at Wasioja, of which he is Principal, and to other educational matters in Minnesota.   The question
is, shall Baptists have anything to do in this matter, or shall we let
things take their course, and not attempt to educate our sons and
daughters in our denominational schools?

Prof. TEN BROEK said that it had been said that we have no
religion in the Michigan University.   Do you not remember that one

of the missionaries designated last evening was converted there? It was all a mistake that we can not have religious influence in State institutions.

Prof. JOHN STEVENS gave some reminiscences of Denison University. He thought that the starting out on a grand plan was the making of that school. He was of opinion that the true way for Baptists was to start a college in every one of the larger States; not an academy. The Western people wanted something with a large and high-sounding title. He advocated the wisdom of having colleges in every State, and he would urge their early establishment in all the new States, and rally around them all the strength possible to secure.

Dr. READ, of Minnesota, strongly advocated the commencing our educational work in the new States of the West with colleges and universities, instead of academies. They would be more successful from the beginning. Every ambitious town would subscribe money and lands for a college or university, while they would not look at a proposition to establish an academy. There is something in a name, after all. And then, colleges would create feeders for themselves.

Dr. CUTTING inquired if Dr. READ did not think that the existence of academies would add largely to the number of college students.

Dr. READ replied that it undoubtedly would. He again reiterated that it would be much easier to obtain contributions for a college than for an academy, even of the same grade. People at the West want something that sounds large.

Prof. TEN BROEK, of Michigan, remarked that he need not say how much he admired the paper which had been read, for the clearness and force of its statements. Of all education he thought university education might be most safely obtained by Baptists in State institutions. By the time the student reaches that stage, he has opinions formed and fixed; while in the academy period his views were unformed and immature. He thought that the question of denominational universities had better be indefinitely postponed, that we may expend our efforts on academies and colleges.

Rev. J. N. SEELEY, of Iowa, spoke generally upon the questions before the Convention. He was opposed to Baptists having anything to do with institutions of learning under the patronage of the State.

The Convention then adjourned with prayer by Rev. JAMES UPHAM, D.D., of Massachusetts.

THURSDAY, MAY 25.

MORNING SESSION.

After prayer by Rev. Dr. WOOD, of Upper Alton, the Convention listened to the reading of a paper by Rev. J. BULKLEY, D.D., of Shurtleff College, upon the question:

HOW CHRISTIAN INSTITUTIONS OF HIGHER LEARNING, ACAD-
EMIES, COLLEGES, UNIVERSITIES AND THEOLOGICAL
SEMINARIES, KEEPING PROGRESS WITH THE GROWTH
OF SOCIETY, CAN BEST BE BUILT UP IN THE WEST, WITH
DUE REGARD ALWAYS TO OTHER NECESSARY EXPEND-
ITURES OF MONEY FOR RELIGIOUS PURPOSES.

By the "West" we understand the Northern portion of the Mississippi valley and the regions bordering on these lakes. By "Christian Institutions" we suppose to be meant especially institutions under denominational control. The question propounded is entirely practical and exceedingly difficult. The ability of the church to rise to the measure of her obligation can not be questioned. Her willingness must depend upon her clear perception of recognized obligation. The difficulties in the way of building up these higher institutions are not peculiar to the "West;" if we except perhaps two elements — her youth and her consequent want of large wealth which can only accumulate through the investments of centuries. Time was when elements of Western character were peculiar. The richness of the virgin soil of this valley, the low price at which the most desirable homesteads could be obtained, the salubrity and comparative healthfulness of the climate, the freedom of religious opinions, the essential equality of all classes in social position, and the wonderful opportunities for political pre-ferment, presented strong attractions to those who sought wealth or power, position or honor, a d brought together in this valley, from all parts of the world, elements of character most dissimilar and antagonistic. It has been declared to be a heterogeneous mass without any homogeneous character. Wildest confusion reigned supreme. Even now, every city, town and village is a perfect Babel. Almost every shade of political and religious opinion in the world is firmly held, fearlessly advocated and freely tolerated. It is the crucible, heated seven times hotter than it is wont to be heated, into which the Almighty chemist has cast every conceivable social, political and religious opinion, and the resulting amalgam is as yet by no means determined. Well will it be for the world and church, if in the experiment the crucible itself, by the intensity of its own action, is not rent into a thousand fragments.

But in this respect the West is no longer peculiar. The foundations of society in the old world are broken up. Cherished political and religious institutions are no longer revered simply because their locks are hoary with the frosts of many centuries. Men are demanding their birth-right. The divine right of kings is questioned and denied. The inalienable rights of man are discussed in the very cabinets of kings and emperors. Papal infallibility possesses no power to save a crumbling religious despotism. The "Star of the East" guides the masses as well as the "wise men" to our shores, where freedom to worship God is guaranteed to all, and the teeming millions, in even geometrical ratio, within the last twenty years, have been surging across the Atlantic, filling all the thoroughfares of this new world, flooding the land, and threatening the entire subversion of all our God-given institutions. Ignorance in science, corruption in morals, superstition and infidelity in religion, blast and wither and consume everything valuable, lovely or hopeful. The late war, too, has rocked our continent like the shock of an earthquake. Established and cherished social ideas have been uprooted. New and unexampled energies have been started into life. By one stroke of the pen an entire race has been lifted from slavery to citizenship, and the end is not yet.

These and kindred causes are equalizing the elements of social, political and religious power throughout the entire land, so that there will soon be, literally, no North, no South, no East, no West. Hence the principles that apply to the building up of the "Higher Institutions of Learning" elsewhere apply with equal force in the West It is taken for granted in this paper that our Western institutions, at the earliest possible moment, should be made equal to any in the land. That in all their equipments, in buildings and endowments, laboratories and libraries, chemical and philosophical apparatus, in thoroughness of study and severity of discipline, in the character and culture of our professors and presidents, we must present to young men who seek a liberal education and thorough discipline, attractions equal to those presented by institutions in the East.

First. While we depend upon the masses for the means to meet other and necessary expenditures for religious purposes, we must rely upon the few for liberal contributions to build up these institutions of learning. We speak now exclusively of provisions for buildings, endowments, scholarships, fellowships, etc. Our other religious enterprises, Home and Foreign Missions, the Bible and Publication Societies, the erection of church edifices, and all the necessary church expenses, appeal directly to the consciences and call out the sympathies of the masses. Hence annual, or semi-annual appeals for these religious enterprises can be successfully made, because every one is compelled to acknowledge both their propriety and necessity.

In fact, annual contributions to all our great national societies in perpetuity, and in increased amounts, are becoming to be regarded as an almost indispensable condition of discipleship. The call comes to each with increasing positiveness and power, to make immediate and enlarged provisions for the speedy publication of the Gospel in all lands. Not so in building up these "Higher Institutions" of learning. These appeals must be made to, and dependence placed upon, men of larger cultivation, men who have themselves enjoyed superior literary advantages, and can properly appreciate them, men of more enlarged and liberal views, who can clearly comprehend the immense and undying power exerted by cultivated intellect, men who recognize the fact, patent in all history, secular and sacred, that thoroughly disciplined mind in State and Church controls the world and shapes the destinies of the ages.

Such men, either possessing wealth themselves, or controlling men who do possess such wealth, must guide it into channels flowing liberally and uninterruptedly in the direction of these institutions. Only men of large wealth and liberal culture can be relied on for those really princely donations that are absolutely essential, keeping progress with the spirit of the age, for buildings and endowments, libraries and laboratories, scholarships and fellowships, galleries of science and art, gathering together and preserving in these great centers the intellectual and religious, the scientific and æsthetic treasures of the present and the past. Thus, in past ages, all institutions not under State control have been founded and sustained; thus must they be built up in the future.

Second. In order to effect this object, the principles of Christian steward-ship must be more frequently and more clearly presented by representative men, and more distinctly recognized by all.

In the territory embraced within the legitimate influence of three or four of our leading Western colleges, there is wealth enough, owned in fee simple by our membership, to place at the disposal of each of these colleges, within a twelvemonth, more than half a million of dollars, and that, too, without in the least interfering with the legitimate business of our membership, or taking from their families one article of necessity or even luxury. In Illinois alone there are many Baptist churches which severally own property worth, in the aggregate, more than half a million of dollars. It is not uncommon to find men in our churches worth from fifty thousand to two hundred thousand, or even half a million of dollars. They are men devoted to Christ, men who love their race and love the church, and who are willing to meet all the demands of clearly recognized duty. But by far the greater part of all our membership have yet to learn that in religion and in higher education money is a power and a necessity. Its power is acknowledged in politics, in business, in State and National development; but the Gospel, and everything pertaining to it or growing out of it, must be without money and without price. To mingle money and religion, as to mingle politics and religion, is profanation. Every investment made in religious institutions or higher schools of learning, is regarded as a gift, and the idea of moral obli-gation is of necessity excluded. The consecration of property is hardly regarded as a Christian duty. Hence, too often the most reckless extrava-gance on the part of Christians, and the most hazardous experiments to acquire property, are witnessed. The most abject and cringing subjection to the imperious demands of appetite or fashion, in Christian families, annually consumes its millions. Worldliness, voluptuousness, selfishness, and pride, are cultivated and developed to the utter destruction, in numberless instances, of the sons and daughters of the wealthy.

When will our churches be filled with John P. Crozers, who, while living, invest with princely munificence in the cause of sanctified education, and whose sons, stimulated by parental precept and example, by *their* munificent benefactions stud the diadem of the Redeemer with imperishable jewels.

Third. We should patronize our own schools.

I have no means of determining how large a proportion of our sons and daughters are educated in our own institutions of learning. I believe no other body of professed Christians in the West possess so little adhesive denominational power in education as the Baptists. A very large percentage, especially of our daughters, finds its way into Catholic schools, at the immi-nent risk, not only of their loss to evangelical Christianity, but also at the risk of their bitter antagonism to the truth. The idea of moral and financial support to our own institutions of learning, is often allowed very little weight in determining where son or daughter shall be educated. Even when our own institutions possess superior facilities for the most extensive and thor-ough intellectual discipline, and the moral and religious influences are of the highest and purest character, Christian parents deliberately permit the slighest considerations to determine the choice of son or daughter in the selection of a place of study, often placing them under the control of schools far inferior to our own, and where the danger of shipwreck to faith is imminent and alarming.

A large number of students is a necessary element in the *present pros-·perity* of our higher institutions, and the *prospective prosperity* of these institutions, through the students as Alumni, is absolutely immeasurable. We need every element of Baptist strength. True, possible contingencies may justify a parent in sending to other institutions under evangelical control, in preference to our own, but such contingencies, we believe, are rare indeed. I would greatly prefer that my own children should be entirely deprived of intellectual discipline, and their knowledge confined to the merest rudiments, rather than that they should be subjected to the influence of Catholic schools, where faith in evangelical Christianity may be not only rudely shaken, but ruthlessly uprooted.

Should it be said that our own institutions are inferior to others, we should either demand the proof or meet the assertion with a positive denial. Were it proved beyond the possibility of a doubt, that we are behind others in the extent of our provisions for intellectual culture and discipline, this would simply impose upon us the imperative obligation of sending to our own schools, and of making them, at the earliest possible moment, equal to any in the land, and every way worthy our position, our numbers, our wealth, our principles, our prestige, and our history.

Fourth. We should seek a sharper definition of the boundaries of State authority in matters of higher education, and adhere with rigid inflexibility to the time-honored and cherished Baptist idea of an entire separation of Church and State.

I have no disposition to find fault with that noble band of Baptists in our great metropolis, whose recent acceptance of a lease from the city is considered by many a crime of such magnitude as almost to exclude them from the sympathy and confidence of the great Baptist brotherhood. My own opinion is, that in a great variety of ways our churches are charitable institutions, and our institutions of learning, in desiring exemption from taxation, and in seeking kindred advantages, ask and receive direct aid from the State, without thereby in the least acknowledging the right of the State to control them — aid received, too, in methods universally approved, and differing very little from the principle involved in the action in New York, by so many condemned.

But there is, we think, another and a legitimate field of investigation. The State universally assumes the right, and it is generally conceded, to tax her citizens to any assignable limit to support higher institutions of learning, under State control. Against this assumed right, we enter our solemn protest, though we may stand alone. Christians of different denominations are compelled, by the law of self-preservation, by their fidelity to their children, by fealty to Christ, to exert their utmost endeavors to educate their own sons and daughters, at very great expense in their own institutions of learning. Now, in addition to all this necessary expense, often pressed to the very verge of possibility, requiring the most rigid economy, and the severest industry, what right has the State to compel us to pay a large annual tax, to enable her to afford *free tuition*, not only to the children of the indigent, but also to the sons of the wealthy in these *higher* institutions under State control? True, the State has the right, nay, it is made her duty to provide the best possible facilities for the education of all her subjects to a limited extent. But we respectfully ask-if that limit is not reached long before you arrive at these higher institutions?

The State has also the right, and it is made her duty, to provide most liberally for her unfortunate classes—the blind, the insane, the feeble-minded, —but has the State the right to establish and support, by direct taxation, Normal schools, Agricultural colleges, and higher institutions of learning where tuition is comparatively gratuitous? By this gratuitous tuition they are brought in direct competition with denominational institutions, where the student must pay his own tuition. We believe such an assumption of power is a direct and palpable violation, by the State, of the rights of the governed. Besides, does not the experience of the past few years, and do not the indications in the immediate future show conclusively that the most insidious and plausible principles of infidelity, entrench themselves under the guise of Liberal Christianity, in these State institutions? And are they not widely disseminated by scientific lecturers and travelers, who are supported by State funds, wrung by the stern hand of the law from the pockets of our reluctant yeomanry, who, in scores of instances are thereby rendered unable to aid their own institutions, or even afford the means of liberal culture to their own children?

True, many of our noblest Christian instructors are engaged in teaching in State institutions. While this assumed right of the government is claimed and enforced, it must be the duty of the Church to do all in her power to counteract the teachings of infidelity, by encouraging our best men to aspire to the very first places on boards of instruction in State institutions. Am I asked how far the State should go in providing by law, for the education of her subjects? We believe she should provide the most liberal facilities for the education of all classes, perhaps so far as her high schools. But we think she should stop there, and not assume the right to compel all by taxation to pay for the labors of those scientific lecturers, who fill the minds of the inexperienced and unwary with skepticism, and thus undermine the very foundations of our religion. Tuition in all higher institutions should perhaps be gratuitous, but the voluntary principle alone should be relied on for all funds necessary to establish and support them. The voluntary principle and that alone, we regard as in consistence with the genius of our political institutions, and in harmony with the inalienable rights of man. I may differ in judgment with every member of this Convention, but I sincerely protest against the unjustifiable assumption of power on the part of the State. Its evils, present and prospective, are such as to call for earnest effort to check it.

Permit all evangelical and unevangelical denominations, calling themselves Christians, all Catholics and Jews, Mohammedans and Infidels, Atheists and Pagans, to employ their means and men with unrestricted freedom in building up their own higher institutions of learning, but compel none by tax, to support in institutions higher than the high school, teachers or lecturers, whose instructions and moral privileges they can not oppose. Can the State in justice compel me to pay for the dissemination of principles that I despise? If so, upon what principles of equity is the demand based?

Fifth. Let us cultivate a kindlier feeling between different and apparently rival schools.

In the early settlement of a country, large-hearted and conscientious men, governed by no motives of worldly policy or gain, controlled solely by a desire to widely extend the blessing of sanctified learning, may establish a college or found a Theological school, at a point, which, in the development of the resources of a country, and in the progress of population, may be found at a distance from a great center of wealth and population, of commercial and social power. Large property is secured, remunerative investments made, buildings erected, endowments obtained, friends gathered, alumni increased, and the roots of the institution thrown hundreds of fathoms deep into human hearts and human sympathies; shall we ruthlessly uproot them?

Brethren in New York once tried the experiment on Hamilton, founded in prayers and sacrifices. The only result, aside from ill-feeling engendered, was to make the Institution throw its roots the deeper, and extend its boughs the wider. Hamilton lives, and will live as long as our Government shall exist, and possibly a great deal longer. Higher institutions are not easily removed or destroyed. Their vitality is proverbial. Lessons of adversity often give them increased activity and power.

As in the vegetable world, the storms of winter and the darkness of night are as essential to health and development as the sunshine of summer and the light of day; so seasons of peril call forth friends, develop new resources, and gather round an institution elements of power. These elements of power are, however, too often procured at the expense of Christian fellowship and brotherly love, and hence their cost may greatly exceed their value.

Is there not a better way?

When conflicting interests exist, should they not, as far as possible, be harmoniously adjusted in the spirit of the religion of Christ? Should not prayers and sympathies, efforts and material aid, vigorously combine to make our several institutions all that the future of this great government, and the church of Christ, demand. Instead of turning our guns, France-like, against each other, do not reason and religion unite in urging to a more thorough combination of all our resources to give the widest possible efficiency to all in the contest with an unequal foe?

Institutions of learning, long established and partially endowed, resist with wonderful energy, and almost certain success, every effort to remove or destroy them, by whomsoever made. Said Abram to Lot, "Let there be no strife, I pray thee, between thee and me, and between my herdsmen and thy herdsmen, for we are brethren." Moreover the difficulties in the way of building up our Western institutions do not exist so much in the fact that we have too many such institutions, as in the fact that the number of students bears no adequate proportion to the number of our membership. The Baptists in Illinois number 57,594. How far we may have imbibed the unchristian spirit of the age in regarding children as a calamity rather than a blessing, it is not my province to determine. We suppose the number of children in Baptist families will compare favorably with others, and yet we query whether one thousand pupils of both sexes, from Baptist families in Illinois, can be found in our higher institutions at home and abroad. The fact is painful as it is true, that our neglect of higher culture is almost universal.

The principal reasons for this neglect are four: financial inability; the want of a proper appreciation of the nature and value of intellectual culture; the lack of proper parental authority in requiring children to pursue a course of study; and covetousness.　　　　　－

The first needs no remark. Financial inability effectually excludes thousands from intellectual culture who otherwise would secure it. In regard to the *second*, permit me to say that thousands of Christian parents suppose that six months or a year's study in a commercial college will thoroughly qualify their promising boy to enter immediately the highway to mercantile or professional success, placing him, in the briefest possible period, on the same plane with Drew or Vanderbilt, Astor or Stewart. Nay, if he does not become a gubernatorial, or even presidential possibility, as soon as the period of constitutional eligibility is reached, the parents are disappointed. If Rail-splitters and Tanners can become Presidents, much more those who have been graduated from a commercial college. Tens of thousands of sons and daughters are ruined for time, if not for eternity, by this false system of education, that, in violation of all the established laws of God, would, in a single year, metemorphose a little child into an intellectual giant.

In regard to the third point, it is sufficient to remark that, in numberless instances, parents possess the financial ability and the earnest desire to thoroughly educate their children; but their entire system of family government is so wretchedly defective, that to keep a child for a series of years at hard work in a higher institution of learning, subject to the severest drill of which it is capable, is an impossibility.

In the fourth instance, the love of money, or pure covetousness, effectually excludes from our halls of learning large numbers of the noblest youth of our land, every element of whose being palpitates with desire to thoroughly explore the fields of scientific investigation. In the esteem of covetousness, a few paltry dollars are permitted to outweigh all the advantages arising from thorough culture. True, in subsequent years, the child, under favorable influences, may partially repair the injury sustained, and become respectably intelligent, useful, and happy. But in numerous instances he must go through life, ignorant and painfully conscious of his inferiority; gazing upon all the beauties of God's glorious universe with no taste or ability to enjoy them. But for covetousness he might have been the peer of the ablest and noblest men of the land, walking, as John B. Gough expresses it, " with his foot upon the daisy, and his head among the stars."

Instead, then, of laboring to restrict the influence of institutions already established, let us unitedly and earnestly labor to correct those false and destructive ideas of education, and fill all our colleges to repletion with the sons and daughters of our common brotherhood. This I regard as the most effectual method of building up Western institutions in the shortest practicable period. It is fundamental to our growth and development.

Sixth. Encourage concentration of gifts to the largest possible extent upon our institutions of learning.

No more suicidal policy was ever adopted by a pastor, than that policy that would either discourage, or fail to encourage, the very largest possible benefactions, on the part of the wealthy, fearing that his own salary, or his own church, would suffer to the full amount of all contributions to benevolent objects outside of his own immediate field of labor. The most successful method of drying up all Christian sympathy, and effectually closing all channels of home benevolence, is to confine your gifts to your own field. Teach your people that everything is demanded for home consumption, and you will soon have nothing to consume. But open wide as possible the channels of benevolence for foreign fields, and every necessity of the church at home will be liberally and cheerfully provided for. It is hardly possible, save in very extreme cases, to secure too large benefactions to the church, or to the cause of sanctified education. Hence, one of the very best methods of building up our higher institutions of learning, in harmony with the enlarged demands for money for other religious purposes, is to encourage, not only the most liberal benefactions for home and foreign demands, but to equally encourage the wealthy to concentrate largely upon institutions of learning. The more liberally the wealthy can be induced to give to increase the efficiency and power of our institutions of learning, the more willingly and liberally will they give to meet every other demand of Christian benevolence. It is the stagnant pool that fills the atmosphere with malaria and death. It is the flowing stream, leaping and dancing on its joyous errand to the ocean, that is always full, and that spreads verdure, and beauty, and life, and bliss, around the habitations that skirt its borders.

Hence I have very little sympathy with those who so bitterly condemn the action of our city churches in the erection of these magnificent temples to the worship of the living God, at such immense expense. When will our brethren learn the true philosophy of Christian beneficence? When will they learn that these large-hearted brethren, who give their tens of thousands to the erection of these grand temples, are by these very gifts prepared to honor the largest possible drafts that the cause of Christ may make upon them? Encourage Christian men who are enlightened by the prayerful study of God's Word, and who are directed by the promptings of God's Spirit to give to such causes, and in such amounts as judgment may dictate or ability justify. We need not have the shadow of a fear that the particular cause in which we are so deeply interested will suffer loss by the most enlarged benefactions to other religious purposes.

No investment exerts an influence so extensive and imperishable; none tells with such wonderful power upon the destinies of our race as these large investments made to our colleges and universities. The power thus concentrated and exerted in these great centers of intellectual and religious influence can never die, and falls little short of omnipotence. Very soon, in our own land, under the purely voluntary system, discarding the proffered aid of the State, conferred at the expense of unwarrantable taxation, our higher institutions of learning uniting, in happiest and loveliest wedlock, science and religion, will demand and receive their millions of invested funds from enlightened and consecrated Christian benevolence.

Lastly. Encourage and seek greater personal consecration to Christ. No motive is so legitimate, none possesses such power, as the cross. Stimulus is a necessary condition of active, created intelligence. Great enterprises have their birth and support in great motives, and demand great sacrifices. Immense interests imperiled impose intense, prolonged, and perpetual efforts to save. Man lost becomes man redeemed only through the personal sacrifice of Christ. The value of all these interests must be learned at the cross. At the cross alone can be formed an adequate conception of the future moral greatness and worth of this valley. The teeming millions that are speedily to press Western soil can scarcely be properly estimated. Illinois alone, during the last two decades, has added not far from eight hundred thousand each ten years to her population. She is within herself already a vast empire, and her immense possibilities may well appal the stoutest Christian heart. The unparalleled fertility of Western soil, our inexhaustible mineral resources, the salubrity and healthfulness of our climate, our central position on this continent, and our rapidly-increasing facilities for national and international communication, all present unequaled attractions to native and foreigner.

The West is an immense loadstone, irresistibly attracting its millions from all parts of the globe. Already the wealth of our churches is becoming enormous. Christian men must seek and find channels of investment. They do not wish, they must not expect, to leave all to dissolute heirs. God demands their wealth. The cross pleadingly presents its arms to receive it. The treasury of the Lord upon its knees imploringly asks it. It will not be withheld. The love of Christ will constrain its consecration. Look at the two great central Western cities, Chicago and St. Louis — rival cities, made such by the Deity — great centers of commerce, of wealth, of social and political and religious power, whose every throb is felt to the very extremities of our national life. They must be regenerated. This can only be done through the instrumentality of educated Christian men; hence the absolute necessity for the most enlarged and liberal provisions for intellectual and religious culture. Within a radius of one hundred miles of each of these cities, in a brief period, will be seen a population of ten millions. What shall be their character ? — what their institutions ? — what their destiny ? In all the past the Baptists have been the *pioneers*, as they have been the *supporters*, of civil and religious freedom — the true democracy of earth. Shall they soon fling their banner to the breeze, and inscribe on its folds — "*Freedom to Worship God ?*" Shall social, civil, political, intellectual, religious freedom be the inalienable inheritance of all, without regard to nationality or color or previous condition ? These are great problems, whose solution is in the womb of the future. To aid in their solution is the mission of cultivated Christian men.

Our *propelling* and our *enduring* power must be drawn from the cross of Him "who though He was rich, for our sakes became poor, that we through His poverty might be rich." Christians must more generally have His spirit of consecration ; then will every want of our higher institutions of learning be supplied.

A single thought, in conclusion. Our institutions of learning must be regarded as the very basis of the prosperity of every religious enterprise ; hence they must command the first and best energies of the church, and the largest consecration of property. Every department of Christian enterprise is emphatically, and without qualification, dependent for success upon *men* — *Christian men* — men of large hearts — men of cultivated intellects — men, all of whose energies, influence and wealth are consecrated to the cross. Give us *earnest, intelligent, cultivated, pious Christian pastors*, and a correspondingly *devoted, earnest*, and *thoroughly disciplined* church, and no combination of the powers of darkness can resist our aggressions. Give us men (and women, too) and missions, the Bible and Publication cause, and the various objects of Christian benevolence shall have all the means necessary to speedily fill the world with the knowledge of a crucified and risen Redeemer.

When the Master founded His kingdom He chose not *wealth*, but *men* — men poor in the goods of this world, but rich in faith — men to whom He gave personal instruction for more than three years, "speaking as never man spake," and then sent them forth to found an empire, governed by laws and replenished with resources directly from God. They founded a spiritual empire, destined to undermine and destroy every system of oppression and tyranny on the face of the globe, and lift the nations up into the freedom of the sons of God — into the very sunlight of Heaven.

The subject of the paper was opened for discussion.

Judge WORDING, of South Carolina, wished to express his most hearty concurrence in the sentiments of the paper just read, especially the point that the dependence of the higher institutions of learning must be upon the men of liberal culture who have wealth. He alluded to the warm affection he had always felt for the institution where he had studied. He believed that such experience among the alumni of colleges is common, and that it prepares them to feel an interest in all institutions of higher learning. He also gave his support to the view taken in the paper that we should sustain our own institutions; as likewise that regarding the relations of the State to higher education, dwelling especially upon the influences hostile to evangelical religion, which so often are seen at work in State universities and colleges.

The paper upon Colleges and Universities in the West was at this point referred to the committee to which the subject belongs. The paper of Dr. Bulkley was referred to the Committee on General and Ministerial Education.

Further remarks were made upon the paper of Dr. Bulkley by Rev. J. W. FISH, Dr. L. B. ALLEN, and others.

The following resolution, offered by Dr. WAYLAND, was adopted:

Resolved, That in recommending the publication of the papers presented to this Convention, we do not design to commit ourselves to all the sentiments therein expressed; but that we regard them as clear presentations of the views of their several authors upon important subjects demanding the careful examination of all our people.

The report of the Committee on Delegates was read by the Secretary of the Convention, Rev. Dr. Mitchell. The report was adopted.

The report of the Committee on Academies was then read by the Chairman, Rev. RICHARD M. NOTT, of Illinois:

REPORT OF THE COMMITTEE ON ACADEMIES.

The Committee on Academies, to which was referred the paper by Prof. Stearns on this subject, respectfully report:

This paper we regard, both in respect to its line of argument and its conclusions, as not only able, and of much interest, but also, in the main, as sound and convincing.

The question of academies does not appear to your Committee to be entirely free from difficulties. In different States, it is probable, different circumstances exist, to such an extent that no one rule of policy on this subject will be found applicable unvaryingly everywhere. But certain principles of quite general application can, we think, be laid down.

The subject can be most advantageously approached, perhaps, by beginning with the *college*. The college is recognized as a great existing fact. Now, in order that colleges may be maintained, students must attend them. But it is not a question of maintaining colleges for their own sake. If the welfare of the community is not highly promoted by their existence, let them become extinct. But it is of great consequence to society that there shall be a class of men who have availed themselves of the most complete advantages which experience can devise or money furnish, for the acquisition of the broadest and most thorough culture. For this reason, our colleges and universities should be kept filled with students.

In order that these institutions may constantly and in increasing measure be thus supplied, two things are necessary; one, that opportunities of preparation for college shall be furnished for the benefit of those who desire them; the other, that a greater and more general interest in liberal education shall be cultivated among the people. It is believed by your Committee that to secure these ends, in most, at least, of our States, academies are a necessity. They are required as schools of preparation for college, and as secondary centers of scholarly influence to disseminate a taste for and appreciation of classical learning. Do the preparatory departments connected with many of our colleges suffice for these ends? We think that the negative answer of Prof. Stearns to this question is well supported.

Equally correct, in our judgment, is Prof. Stearns' estimate of the fitness of the High-school system to meet the proposed ends. If it is found in any one of our States, or in any part of a State, that the high-schools are adequate for these important purposes, then academies will not, for these objects, be there needed. But is it not ordinarily the case that unless the principal of the school is himself, not only a liberally educated man, but a sort of enthusiast for liberal learning, positive encouragement will not be furnished to any great extent by the high-schools to the prosecution of studies preparatory to college ? The prevailing sentiment of the community necessarily directs, for the most part, the plans of these schools. Tax-payers often find fault if they have to pay to support, in a public institution, a a system of advantages of which only a very few will be ever inclined to avail themselves. Though a department of preparation for college may be tolerated in these schools, yet they can usually exert but little influence to mould the public sentiment in favor of the education furnished by colleges. But an academy, if it is maintained at all, will almost of necessity exercise such an influence. It is rarely originated that it may be an end to itself as a school, but that it may occupy a subordinate relation to the system of college education. Professedly, it is to the college, what the grammar-school is to the high-school. A pride in the dignity of their institution will of itself be a motive to the founders and instructors of an academy, to keep the classes which are in course of preparation for college as full as they can.

Another consideration favorable to academies is, that they furnish advantages for our agricultural population, which are not accessible to them by any other means. A prosperous academy, which is situated in one of the smaller cities of Illinois, derives its patronage, not chiefly from the citizens, but mostly from the thriving rural districts around. The sons and daughters of the farmers have no high-schools. They can find cheap board at the academy, and enjoy there the finest privileges of study. Many a youth who, after harvest, seeks that seminary with the intention of devoting a single winter, perhaps, to the study of higher mathematics and natural philosophy, becomes so influenced by the literary atmosphere of the place, that he quickly imbibes a desire for liberal learning, and finds himself, after a twelvemonth or more, in college, where he never would have come, but for the impulse thus received.

The religious and denominational argument on the side of academies adds weight to these considerations. Your Committee professes hearty sympathy with, and love of, our public school system. But it is a fact, that the public schools can not, in a great number of instances, be controlled, to

the degree that appears desirable, by the spirit of religion. Here, too, it is
the governing sentiment of the community that rules, and that sentiment is
not often in favor of a very active and prominent religious influence in these
schools. If parish-schools, as a substitute — in the hands of the religious
part of the community — for the common schools, are not a desideratum;
and your Committee thinks they are not; yet, why should not a few institutions, of the grade next lower than colleges, be supported by Christians,
in which their youth may have the benefits of a truly Christian training,
while pursuing the rudiments of a liberal education? It is easy, comparatively, to secure a religious character for an academy. Its founders have
only to keep this steadily in view.

Besides, this Educational Convention consists of Baptists. It is not with
the interests of education in general, so much as with the interests of
education as connected with our duties and our prospects of growth as a
denomination, that we have to do. The colleges which we call upon the
denomination to favor, patronize and build up, are denominational. How
shall we maintain these? How shall we supply them with students? Where
shall we train the young men who have an inclination to prepare themselves
for our colleges? How shall we most efficiently create an influence which
shall not only generate in the minds of youths who are indifferent, or
averse, to a college education, an inclination towards that course of study,
but which shall also win them into *our* colleges? Do we not need some
Baptist academies at important centers in our different States? The pupil
is apt to be influenced by his preceptor in his choice of a college. It is no
unheard-of thing for Baptist lads, in Pedobaptist academies, particularly if
converted there, to become Pedobaptists, and even Pedobaptist ministers.
Would not Baptist academies be an important help in the extension of
Baptist influence, and have some effect in aiding us to reply practically to
the question, How shall we keep the ranks of the Baptist ministry recruited?

Your Committee recognizes fully the need of the soundest sagacity and
most cautious discretion in all that pertains to the business of actually
founding an academical system in any part of the country. Questions of
the most appropriate location, of the probable means of endowment, of the
relation which would be sustained to existing systems of schools, whether
public or private, would have to be wisely, candidly and thoroughly pon-
dered. Neither would the Committee be in favor of an attempt to multiply
rapidly the number of our academies. To aim at anything like "an academy
in every county" would be, indeed, an absurdity. Two or three well-
endowed, well-manned institutions of this order are infinitely preferable, in
the largest, even, of the States, to a dozen or more of such schools, not
efficiently provided for in money and half-officered. Let our resources,
wherever we begin, be concentrated upon one of these undertakings. Let
one academy be rendered vigorous, strong, solid. Then, if another is
needed, proceed to bring that into the same condition. Possibly, in some
States the work would be best begun if one or two colleges should alter
their curriculum of study to an academical scale, and change their titles to
correspond with facts.

[The report thus presented, was recommitted, and afterwards offered
again with the following addition, and then adopted as a whole.]

In conclusion, your Committee calls attention once more to the remark
in the introductory part of the report, that in different States circumstances
differ; and a theoretical argument in favor of academies, even if sound
abstractly, may be practically inapplicable in some regions. We add that

in our opinion it would be highly impolitic to attempt the establishment of Baptist academies in any circumstances in which attention would thus be diverted injuriously from the work of securing endowments for our struggling colleges and theological seminaries.

Respectfully submitted,

R. M. Nott,
A. Owen,
Geo. Kline,
D. H. Cooley,
A. S. Hutchins,
I. N. Carman,
L. B. Allen, D.D.

The report was accepted, and the question of its adoption being before the Convention,

Dr. GREGORY, of Illinois, expressed the belief that, however it may be in the East, here in the West there is a tide of public interest and tendency which is carrying that part of the work of education which is intermediate between the common school and the college into the hands of the high schools. He expressed it as his belief that it is impracticable to establish throughout these States academies which will do efficiently this work of intermediate education. Even if the academy is first upon the ground, the high school when it comes supplants it, while if the academy is founded where the high school already exists, it is sure to fail. The academy is not in accordance with the genius of our people. Our strong and intelligent and wealthy citizens prefer the high school.

Dr. SHEPARDSON, of Ohio, dissented from the last speaker. He instanced the case of Cincinnati, in which it is admitted that the academical schools in that city have fostered and helped public schools. Why is it that the Catholics can sustain ecclesiastical schools of the academical grade, and we not able to do the same? We are able.

Dr. CUTTING also dissented from the view taken by Dr. Gregory. He desired to see the high schools prosper, as well as the State universities. Yet he did not think that the high school necessarily supplants the academy, or tends that way. In Massachusetts, although the high schools are highly prosperous, there never was a time when the academies were so much so.

The report was recommitted with instructions to modify it so as that it shall distinguish between States where academies are of much importance and those where they are not so.

The Convention then listened to a paper by President KENDALL BROOKS, D.D., of Michigan, upon —

THE DUTIES OF THE CHURCHES WITH REFERENCE TO THE PERPETUATION, INCREASE, AND EDUCATION OF THE MINISTRY.

Some things may be taken for granted in the discussion of this subject.

1. There must be a ministry. Christ's appointment, no less than the demands of the church and the world, require that to some men must be assigned the special duty of preaching the Gospel and serving as Christian pastors. While every believer must exert his personal influence for the conversion of sinners, and must in many ways work and sacrifice for the advancement of the church and the honor of Christ, some men must recognize it as their vocation to preach Christ, to lead in every Christian enterprise, to expound and maintain Christian truth, to press the claims of religion on the notice of men, in private as well as in public, — to be Christian ministers.

2. It may also be assumed that the Great Head of the Church calls into the ministry those whom He intends for this service, and that no man, however gifted, however educated, however zealous, ought to take this work upon himself without the call of God.

3. But it may also be assumed that the churches, or the Christians composing them, have some responsibility in reference to the supply of ministers; that those who are called of God to the service sometimes disregard the call; that if the church employs suitable means for preparing and introducing into the ministry those to whom the divine call comes, some will enter on the work who would otherwise turn to other pursuits, and that the number and efficiency of ministers will depend in some measure on the views and efforts and energy of the churches in reference to the increase of such laborers. If a body of Christians, however numerous and powerful, hold as an essential doctrine that inasmuch as God will provide His own ministers, it is an impertinence for men to concern themselves with finding and encouraging and preparing candidates for the ministry, they will have but few ready to assume the work, and these few will be poorly equipped for the warfare. On the other hand, if a body of Christians feel specially called on to pray for an increase in the number of ministers, to look out from among their young men such as give promise of usefulness in this work, to encourage them with sympathy, and to provide for their preparatory training, such a people will be likely to find the ranks of their ministry filling up, and filling with efficient workers. More than a generation ago, one of our churches in the city of Boston had among its members a greater number of young men preparing for the ministry than all the other Baptist churches of the city taken together. When the question was asked how this came to pass, the answer was readily given. The pastor had made special efforts to find such gifts; he had habitually prayed in public that God would raise up ministers, and would honor that church as the mother of many ministers; he had accustomed his people to keep this in view; he had compelled every young man in his church to consider the question of personal duty in reference to preaching, and the result was such as might have been expected. The church, then, has some responsibility in reference to increasing the number of ministers.

That responsibility begins to be met when we begin to pray the Lord of the Harvest to send laborers into the harvest. But this is only the beginning; we fulfill our duty when we work as well as pray.

5

To discuss all our duty in this matter during the short time allotted to this paper would be impossible. Let me therefore call attention to one great duty, the proper performance of which implies or involves all the rest, while I suggest *the kind of education we need to provide* for those who are.to be the pastors of our churches and preachers of the Gospel. When we clearly perceive what education our ministers need, we shall of course see our obligation to provide facilities for acquiring such an education, and to aid in supporting young men while they are acquiring it.

But let us first distinctly recognize the truth, that there is no one standard of preparation to which all must conform. While personal piety and the call of God are essential for every minister, these are the only qualifications that are always, and everywhere, indispensable. A man in whom these two are found may be a useful minister of Jesus Christ, even if he has no human learning and can not spell out God's promises on the sacred page; and from this least educated minister, through all the grades of intellectual attainment to the most thoroughly trained scholar, there are men whom God honors with success as His servants in the ministry of reconciliation. We may expect there will be in all the coming ages, as there have been in all the past, men summoned in mature life from the farm or the forge, from the store or the workshop, to serve Christ in the pulpit; and until vastly larger provision is made for training young men for the ministry, we must continue to pray that the supply from these sources continue. But do we need any argument to prove that another class of ministers is also required, and that those whom God calls in their youth to make preparation for serving Him in the pulpit are called to a different kind of preparation? Many to whom the call of God comes while they are young, disregard it, or fail to make suitable preparation for the work. He can supply the service which these fail to render, and furnish the supply in such way as to make it apparent that the growth of His kingdom is not wholly dependent on human learning. But this divine power and readiness to meet the deficiency can not affect the duty of those who are called in youth to prepare for service as preachers of Christ and teachers of the churches. It can not therefore affect the question of the duty of the Church in reference to the education of these; and it is these whom I wish now to keep in mind, while I speak of the kind of education we ought to provide for candidates for the Christian ministry. Many will enter the ministry and serve Christ faithfully without this education. Many will avail themselves in part of this offered education. Many who desire to obtain it will fall short of the full acquisition. But the question for us is — "What kind of education ought we to provide for those whom God summons to prepare for the great work of preaching Christ?"

I. I say then, first, that we need to provide an education which includes, as a primary element, *mental discipline.* Ministers have some work to do which none but men of well-trained minds can efficiently perform. They are the public defenders of the truth; they are expositors of the Word of God; they must meet error in a thousand forms, and constantly in new forms. It is not enough for them to have learned from text-books the arguments with which unbelievers of a former age assailed the doctrines of Christianity, and the answers to those arguments; they must have such power of mind, acquired by rigid discipline, as will enable them to meet new arguments, to see and expose new errors, and to adapt themselves to all the forms of assault to which the truth is exposed. They must be able to investigate for themselves questions which were not so much as stated when they were in the seminary, and to analyze doctrines which had not then been announced.

In resisting teachers of false doctrine, and in removing difficulties which trouble disciples or honest inquirers, the minister needs clearness of perception, and logical power, and readiness and vigor of intellect—qualities which indeed imply original capacity, but which are greatly increased by long and laborious discipline. The Divine Master showed His estimate of such qualifications for the ministry when he laid His hand on the clear-headed, logical, and well-trained Saul of Tarsus, and made him the chief champion of Christianity in its first encounter with the world. How could the apostle have fulfilled his mission if he had lacked those powers of mind which rigorous discipline develop ? How could he have set forth before the cavilling Jews, with unanswerable argument, the claims of Jesus as the Messiah, and proved to the wise men of Athens the divine origin of Christianity, so that they could not resist his logic ? And in our times a minister who can not detect fallacies and distinguish between the specious and the real, and give a reason for the faith he holds, must often be put to shame in the presence of new forms of unbelief.

A preacher who has been exhibiting the way of salvation through Christ, and trying with an earnest zeal to persuade men to walk in that way, when he has left the pulpit, is met by a man whose conscience is somewhat aroused, but who excuses himself from being a Christian by some objection he has heard urged against the divine authority of the Bible Such objections are always assuming new forms, and this assumes a form which the preacher has never met before. If he can readily take it to pieces and show the error that is mingled with the truth; if he can see, and cause his friend to see, that it is an unsound argument, depending for its force on some falsehood tacitly assumed to be true, or on some distortion of the truth, he can tear away the refuge of lies and leave the man's conscience to feel the full force of the earnest appeal. Oh! how many a minister has longed for that power, while his burning love for souls and hearty devotion to Christ have not been able to compensate for its absence, but have only made him feel his need more keenly. How many a minister has groaned bitterly in spirit for lack of that power of analysis and argument which the rigid discipline of the schools would have given him. In the ardor of his youth he thought it was only necessary to tell men the story of Christ's love and persuade them to receive the grace of God. Therefore he turned away from the course of study which seemed so long, and hastened to assume his ordination vows. In his maturity, when experience has proved his mistake and his increasing years make the mistake irreparable, he does not cease to regret that he entered on this warfare so inadequately equipped for the conflict.

Ministers whose mental discipline is comparatively small are not useless. It is a most cheering thought that they labor in the service of one who can employ the weakest means for accomplishing glorious results, and who has often honored himself by causing the foolish things of the world to confound the wise, and weak things to confound the mighty, and base and despised things, and things that are not, to bring to nought things that are. But that fact does not encourage weakness in the pulpit, any more than it encourages foolishness in the pulpit. The most thoroughly disciplined mind is, with all its original and acquired strength, always weak enough to illustrate the power of God in using it for His glory. We need not be afraid of taking from our Lord the honor of working through instruments which, without His efficiency, would be utterly powerless. It is our part to employ in His service our noblest faculties, most fully developed and matured and strengthened for the work assigned us. And He will delight to employ such powers, even as He delights in the consecration to himself of the best affections and the richest gifts.

Moreover, ministers of the Gospel greatly need that breadth of view, that largeness of mental grasp, that power to rise above the influence of prejudice, which come naturally from generous mental discipline. The power to see whatever of truth there is in any teachings, however mingled with error, and whatever of error there is in any system of doctrines which seems to rest on fundamental truth, is a most desirable power for a religious teacher. The value of such a power is illustrated in nearly all the great leaders of the Church from Paul to Döllinger. It is illustrated in the enlarged influence of many a Christian pastor who has disarmed opposition by his readiness to acknowledge truth wherever he has found it, and to admire Christian character exhibited by men who had not learned all the truth of Christ. Now a generous Christian charity may dwell in one who has enjoyed no large opportunities for mental discipline. But as it is the tendency of such discipline to enlarge the mental powers, to increase the range of vision, and to lift above the influence of prejudice,—ministers of the Gospel, who are ambassadors of the broad-minded Christ, may well seek such discipline that they may more faithfully represent their glorious Lord. The tendencies of human nature are to narrowness. Even those men who claim to be the special champions of free thought, and whose liberalism consists chiefly in utter indifference to truth. are so narrow in their sympathies and fellowship that they seem to feel supreme contempt for all who are not of their own narrow circle, and especially they can not tolerate anything so definite and positive as the teachings of Jesus. But if any man can afford to be broad in his views and all-reaching in his charity, it is the man who knows that he holds the truth as it is in Jesus; the truth which will ultimately triumph, as surely as the kingdom of God prevails among men. Baptists are sometimes stigmatized as narrow-minded, because they are said to stand on so narrow a platform as the mere form of an external ordinance. But inasmuch as we know that our platform is the broadest possible for Christians—simple allegiance to Christ, personal, all-pervading allegiance to Him as our teacher and Lord—we can not afford to be narrow-minded; we are under obligations to be broad-minded; our ministers, the representatives of our faith before the world, ought to learn to take broad views In preparing for the ministry they may well seek that discipline of the mind which enlarges its grasp, makes its vision clearer and wider, and extends its sympathies to all that is good and true.

II. I pass on to observe, secondly, that we need to provide for our ministers an education which includes thorough and ample *learning*. The mental discipline which has been urged may be acquired without much learning. It is rather the preparation for learning, and the means by which learning is to be acquired through all the years of a man's life. He is not a well-educated man, who has simply learned whatever of science or literature is taught in the college course, and thinks he needs to learn nothing more. His time has largely been spent in acquiring skill to use the instruments which he will need hereafter in the acquisition of learning, and in the investigation of truth. But the minister, when he enters on his work, needs something more than merely preparation for efficient study. He needs learning in the very beginning of his public service. He announces himself as an expounder of the truth of God. His work as a preacher is to interpret, and exhibit, and illustrate, and apply the word of God. He needs to have studied that word carefully, laboriously, prayerfully, with all the best helps at his command, under the direction of men who make it their life-work to shed light upon the sacred page. The Bible is the guide-book of immortal souls in their journey through this world. Shall any man assume to publish its instructions until he has used suitable means of assuring himself that he reads them aright? Is there any amount of learning which a man may not desire, if he is to set forth before his fellow-immortals the plan of God for saving sinners? That plan is indeed so simple that the unlearned may understand it, if he desires. But the minister must preach to those who do not desire to. He must prove to the unwilling hearer that the Bible is a revelation from God. He must demonstrate the authoritative claims of Jesus Christ as teacher and Lord. He must prove the falseness of all the systems of belief which go under the name of Christianity but are destitute of its essential characteristics. He must show what the teachings of the Bible are, in reference to the character and condition of men, and the way of salvation for sinners. Will not learning help to prepare him for these duties? The more thoroughly he has studied the languages in which the Scriptures were written, the better prepared he will be to expound those Scriptures and hunt out the error that has hidden itself in dark passages. The more diligently he has explored the Scriptures, the more fully will he be prepared to state, and exhibit, and defend the doctrines which they teach. The more study he has expended on the evidences of Christianity, the more confident will he be of the truth of the Bible, and the more successful in convincing other men of its truth. The more he has compared doctrine with doctrine, and examined each truth in its relation to every other, the more clear will be his conception of the different truths, and the more symmetrical and compact the whole system of Christian truths will appear to him; and therefore he will be able rightly to divide the word of God, and to exhibit Christian truth as complete, harmonious, perfectly adapted to the wants of men.

Our conception of an efficient, thoroughly-prepared minister of the Gospel includes, in addition to all natural and spiritual qualifications, learning, generous and ever-increasing. And, for such a man, no learning can be useless which will help him in his work. Not only the languages in which the Bible was written, but all literature, ancient and modern,— not only theology as a science, but all the sciences, unfolding the laws of God, and showing the glory of God,— not only the history of the Church, but all history as illustrating the Providence of God;— come within the range of the Christian scholar's study, and by them all he may acquire new power to defend the truth, and convince men, and serve the church, and glorify Christ.

He can not have all learning when he begins to be a minister, nor indeed ever. But the more he has in the beginning, the stronger he will be for his work, and the more likely to make further acquisitions. Every young man, burning with desire to be a good minister of Jesus Christ, may well wish to acquire learning, that he may fulfill more efficiently the ministry committed to him. And the more learning he has, the more may he delight to bring it as an offering to be laid at the Master's feet.

III. A third essential element in the education which our ministers need, is that *culture* by which learning and mental power are made most effective in the pulpit. Of course culture comes in connection with mental discipline and learning. These can not exist without some measure of it. But then great strength of intellect is not always joined with those graces of style and that power in speech which give to a man favor with the people. The preacher must first have something to say; but he must also know how to say it, and have power to say it. A very learned man is sometimes an inefficient man in the pulpit, because he can not express his thoughts clearly, freely, and forcibly. Many a great man has found himself less effective as a preacher than his brother of far smaller endowments, because the one has facility of expression, and a cultivated voice, and an attractive or impressive manner, while the other delivers his great thoughts as if it were no concern of his, whether his people feel their force, or understand them, or even hear them. A great many preachers are criminally destitute of this element of power. They seem to think it a sign of weakness to pay much regard to the dress of thought, or to spend much time in acquiring an easy and forcible delivery; as if anything could be unimportant which can secure the attention of men to the claims of God and to their own permanent welfare and character. We are all, even the most advanced among us, greatly affected by these things in a speaker. It detracts from our interest in his thoughts if, through lack of effort on his part, we are compelled to exert ourselves to hear the words which he ought to utter distinctly. We inevitably suspect the validity of his arguments, or the accuracy of his facts, if he offends the ear with vicious pronunciations, or is careless and slovenly in his grammatical constructions. We are provoked to laughter by uncouth gestures and awkward postures. We do not like to be persuaded by one who vociferates when nothing demands a vehement utterance, or who pours forth such volumes of sound as quite drown all articulate words. A pleasing voice, completely under the control of the speaker; an earnest manner which shows that the man is himself thoroughly interested in what he says; an easy movement which makes the hearers feel that the speaker is at home in his work; appropriateness of inflection and gesture, as far removed from affectation as from awkwardness; freedom from professional tone and offensive mannerism; directness, and clearness, and vivacity of style; fulness, and force, and beauty of illustration; power to awaken the sympathy of all who hear; — these are acquisitions which no minister of the Gospel is at liberty to hold in light esteem. They are an important part of his preparation for his work. To neglect them is to be untrue to the Lord who has called him to preach the Gospel; it is to be unfaithful to the immortal men to whom he is commissioned to speak in the Master's name.

This third element in the education our ministers need is more likely to be neglected than either of the others, while it is more easy of acquisition. It is only an outward thing, yet, in proportion to the time and labor required for securing it, is more valuable to the minister than great vigor of intellect, or large stores of learning.

What, then, is the duty of our churches in reference to the perpetuation, increase, and education of the ministry?

We answer briefly:

1. To establish and maintain schools in which our young men may have opportunity for the most thorough mental training; — not theological seminaries alone, not colleges alone, but these in connection with schools of lower grade. We can not fulfill our duty in reference to the future ministry, unless we have institutions of learning, of all grades, of the very best character. The foundation must be well laid. Faithful, enthusiastic, thorough teachers must be employed in the lowest schools. And here we come again upon the truth so fully recognized already, that one of our greatest wants is a considerable number of preparatory schools in which the best instruction may be given, and the foundation be laid for generous scholarship, and large growth in mental power. Mental discipline must be acquired mainly in the academy and the college. The theological school has no time for this work. It receives young men who are supposed to be already well trained, in prepar-

ation for theological study. If they have not had the discipline of the college, or such discipline acquired elsewhere, the theological course must bring far less advantage to them than it ought to bring. Our colleges must mainly furnish the discipline of our candidates for the ministry. Let the churches see to it that these institutions are well sustained, provided with able and enthusiastic teachers, and filled with young men called of God to serve Him in the ministry.

2. Our second duty is to make ample provision for the acquisition of theological learning. For this the theological seminary is demanded. It must be planned on a broad scale; must furnish a generous course of study; must have broad-minded, earnest, inspiring, godly scholars for its teachers, enough of them to do the work most thoroughly; and, withal, the churches must encourage their young men to repair to it for study. Saying nothing about other institutions, we have occasion to thank God, as well as congratulate ourselves, that the foundations of such a school have been laid here,—that men of ample endowments and generous enthusiasm, growing riper every year, have been called into its service, and have already given proof of their call from God to this work. Let the endowment be completed as soon as possible. Let the vacant chairs be filled by other men of equal capacity, and attainments, and aptness to teach. Let the library be filled with all literature that can help in the study of the Bible, or in preparation for the work of a minister. Let this school have our warmest sympathy and most generous support; and year by year it will gather the young men from our colleges, and nourishing them in all the elements of ministerial power through the three favored years of their study here, it will send them forth in consecrated companies, to preach salvation by Jesus Christ, to guide the churches, to strengthen the faith of believers, to win sinners to holiness, and to hasten the coming of that blessed era when the whole earth shall rejoice in the established reign of Christ.

3. A third duty is that our schools of learning, both colleges and seminaries, shall give special attention to the training of young men for their work in the pulpit. Every college, and especially every theological school, should make adequate provision for instruction in elocution, for training the voice, and for cultivating all those powers of rhetoric and oratory by which the truth as uttered by the preacher is made effective and irresistible. Whatever else fails, this should be provided.

4. A fourth duty, resting on us all, is to aid in supporting those whom God calls to prepare for the ministry. Most of them, by a wise appointment, are poor men, that they may better serve the poor as well as the rich. They need encouragement, and sympathy, and money. Let our education societies be generously supported, and no young man ever be allowed to suffer for the comforts of life while he is seeking preparation for the ministry, as some have suffered who have gone before him, and as some perhaps are suffering now. Every church, the small as well as the large, ought, once in every year, to make a contribution as God has prospered it, for helping those young brethren who have turned away from secular pursuits to spend their lives in the ministry of the Gospel.

These are our duties, brethren. They are serious and weighty, but not altogether unwelcome duties. Not reluctantly, not as a sacrifice, but with glad earnestness, let us do all this work, thanking God that He permits us to bear a part in so glorious an enterprise.

Prof. STEVENS said he had been trying to work up the Baptists of Ohio to meet the wants of the ministry.

Rev. F. A. DOUGLASS, of Ohio, spoke at some length upon the necessity of sending out cultivated missionaries to India.

Rev. Dr. FYFE, of Woodstock, Canada, spoke of the educational interest in Canada. If the Baptists had as many young men studying for the ministry as Canada had, in proportion to their membership, there would be 5,500 theological students in the Baptist colleges of the United States.

Rev. J. C. C. CLARKE, of Ohio, made some earnest and impressive remarks upon the danger of ordaining men too suddenly for the ministry.

The paper was referred to the Committee on the Increase of the Ministry and Theological Education.

On motion of Rev. Dr. CUTTING, the following resolutions were passed.

Resolved, That the thanks of this Convention are due and are tendered to the First Baptist Church, in Chicago, for the use of their house of worship, and to the members of that church and congregation, and to other Christian friends, for the hospitalities of their homes.

Resolved, That the proceedings of this Convention be printed under the supervision of the Secretary, with any necessary advice of the Western Advisory Committee of the American Baptist Educational Commission.

Resolved, That the thanks of the Convention are due to Messrs. Church and Goodman, of Chicago, for assuming the responsibility of the publishing of the proceedings, and the pastors and other friends of education are earnestly desired to promote their wide circulation by forwarding orders for copies to Messrs. Church and Goodman, "Standard" office, Chicago.

The Chairman of the Committee on Academies reported further an addition to their report recognizing the different circumstances found in different States, with reference to the existing need of academies. The report was adopted.

Pending its adoption, Rev. A. OWEN, of Michigan, spoke of it as an important element in this question, that what are now new States will in time be old States, and that what old States have learned to do, new States will in time reach. He believed that academies will become a necessity in States where at present they seem not to be needed. He referred to the work done by academies in some of the older States, as that of New London, in New Hampshire, as illustrating what an important sphere they may be expected one day to fill in the educational system of the West.

Rev. Dr. L. B. ALLEN, of Minnesota, felt deeply interested in the religious aspect of the question. He was persuaded that a proper consideration of this subject would carry the Convention in favor of academies. ..He referred to incidents in his own experience, going to show the important influence exerted in academical schools in this direction. Service of this kind can not be expected of high schools. He alluded to another fact, that in Minnesota there is at present no school, whatever, properly under the patronage of the Baptists. Schools of the class now considered may supply such deficiency in States where colleges are as yet impracticable.

The Convention adjourned with singing, to meet at 2 P.M.

AFTERNOON SESSION.

The Convention was opened with prayer by Rev. ALFRED OWEN, of Michigan.

The motion pending at the adjournment was one adopting the report of the Committee on Academies.

Dr. WAYLAND moved that this report, and all other reports of committees, be accepted and printed without discussion.

Dr. CUTTING hoped the motion would not prevail. There are important matters in some of the reports which ought to be discussed. An adoption without the discussion would defeat some of the objects of this Convention.

After some further discussion, Dr. WAYLAND withdrew his motion, and the question recurred upon the adoption of the report of the Committee on Academies.

The report was adopted.

The report of the Committee on Colleges and Universities was then read by the Chairman, Rev. A. N. ARNOLD, D.D., of Illinois.

REPORT OF COMMITTEE ON COLLEGES AND UNIVERSITIES.

Your Committee on Colleges and Universities, to whom the paper presented last evening by Dr. J. A. Smith was referred, ask leave to present the following report:

They find that in the portion of our country which falls properly within the view of this Convention, the Baptist denomination has *eleven* higher institutions of learning, bearing the name of College or University. Of this number Iowa has *three*, Illinois *two*, and Michigan, Ohio, Indiana, Missouri, Kansas, and Wisconsin, one each. *Six* of these have fairly reached the rank of colleges, namely, *two* in Illinois, and one in each of the States of Michigan, Ohio, Indiana, and Missouri.

The common need of all is a large addition to their endowments; and the chief obstacle to the adequate increase of their endowments is not so much the poverty of our people in the regions on which they chiefly depend for their support, nor the excess of their number above the real wants of the communities in which they are located, as the want, on the part of our Baptist people, of a due sense of the value and need of a higher education. The importance of building up these institutions, to the extent of one in each State, to the stature of well-endowed colleges, with a broad curriculum of study, ample libraries, and all needful appliances for scientific illustration and investigation, can hardly be exaggerated. If, in the newer and more sparsely peopled States, colleges can not be brought up to this high standard at once, it should be the persistent and hopeful aim of those to whom their management is entrusted, to advance them as steadily and as speedily as possible towards this goal. We say hopeful, as well as persistent aim; for the history of the educational institutions of our country has afforded many signal examples to show that the feeblest beginnings of Christian faith may grow into strong and majestic consummations. The duty of the hour, in the judgment of your Committee, is to give earnest attention to the enlargement and improvement of our *Colleges*, leaving the great *Universities* of the future to be shaped as the wants and the wisdom of the future may dictate.

Your Committee, in closing their report, would sum up their convictions in the following resolutions :

Resolved, That we express our devout gratitude to Almighty God, that our denominational colleges have been to so great an extent pervaded by Christian influences, and so often visited by the converting grace of His spirit; and that we regard the continuance of this blessing as indispensable to our highest denominational prosperity, and to the adequate supply of our churches with an educated and godly ministry.

Resolved, That we recognize our duty, as Christian educators and as Baptists to do what we can to bring our wealthy laymen to a just appreciation of the duty and privilege of devoting a generous portion of their wealth to the better endowment of our denominational colleges.

Respectfully submitted,

A. N. ARNOLD, *Chairman.*

Dr. GREGORY spoke decidedly in favor of the adoption of the report. He had been pained with the depressed condition of the Baptist educational interest in the West. He had been thinking whether a crusade could not be aroused in favor of these institutions. He wanted to throw it out that instead of going into the field — instead of coming down to us for one institution — come down with all the power that can be derived from a general consideration of Baptist Educational interests. He believed a movement could be inaugurated here to-day which would give to the aid of Baptist institutions from one million to a million and a half of dollars. He would have an appeal in Christ's name, an appeal to the Christians of the Northwest, go out among the people in aid of this work, that such men as Dr. Burroughs and Dr. Wayland might be relieved from a work which is crushing them. Let us all bear it — or, at least, our portion of it.

Dr. STONE deprecated the practice of decrying the number of colleges now in existence. Though there might be some weak ones, yet we have none too many. The only fault is, we do not sustain them as we ought, or as we might. He proceeded at some length to show that our colleges are mostly local institutions.

Rev. LUTHER STONE, of Chicago, followed the same line of thought, and gave carefully prepared statistics, which abundantly proved his positions. And, in this respect, our denominational institutions are not singular.

Rev. A. OWEN, of Michigan, did not coincide with the idea that we should have a college in every State. He hoped that this Convention would take no steps to set our brethren in the new States about any such business. They had had an experience in Michigan which they would not like to repeat. In regard to those already established, he would be the last one to tear them down.

Prof. MITCHELL, of Chicago, said that the clause in the report which Bro. Owen opposes, was one which he approved, but with a different interpretation. He thought the recommendation to mean that they should have one college for every State, as a maximum, and not have two or three. He did not understand either that it was proposed to go about the establishment of these colleges at once. Prof. Mitchell described the policy which had been pursued by the Congregationalists, and hoped we might improve them.

Rev. J. T. WESTOVER was emphatically in favor of the sentiments of the report presented by Dr. Arnold. He gave at some length the reasons for having one college in each State. He thought the theory of the paper read last night very beautiful, but impracticable and inapplicable in practice. He therefore decidedly approved of the plan of one college to a State, so far as the West was concerned.

The report was adopted.

The Convention then listened to a paper by Rev. J. V. SCHOFIELD, of Iowa, upon

THE CARE OF EDUCATION, AS PART OF PASTORAL DUTY; WITH THE BEARING OF A GENERAL AND EFFECTIVE MOVEMENT IN EDUCATION ON THE CHARACTER, PROGRESS, AND USEFULNESS OF THE DENOMINATION.

In Germany, the pastor is designated as " He who has the care of souls." This designation implies a care in education.

The pastor brings souls to Christ by teaching them the gospel, and leads them to fullness in Christ by continued and more complete instruction.

The derivation of his official title imposes upon him the duty to guide, to nourish. He does this by religious teaching, and by guiding the disciples, the flock, into spiritual pastures (Eph. iv, 11). So understood the Apostle when he wrote, "To some he gave pastors and teachers." The best expositors are agreed that both words refer to the one office of pastor. The commission makes the pastor pre-eminently a teacher. He is first to teach, then baptize. He is more a Samuel than an Aaron. Thus religious education becomes a necessary part of pastoral duty.

Vinet says, "Christianity is a thought of God, which is destined to become a thought of man." If so, pastor and people must understand the word, and teach it. Piety being equal, educated minds can best instruct others in religion. The colleges of our country are the best schools to give a complete education. Their course of study is founded upon the progressive experience of centuries in teaching. Institutions of learning, then, of all grades, and especially colleges and theological seminaries, are necessarily included in a pastor's care.

He need not shrink from this work because of skeptical tendencies in schools of learning. Ignorance produces more infidelity than learning. The majority of our colleges were founded by Christian people, and nearly all their teachers gladly learn of Christ.

Teachers and pastors like Wickliffe, Tyndale, Calvin, Robert Hall, Wesley, Edwards and Dwight, have exhibited a beautiful blending of growth in learning with growth in piety.

Prof. Tyler says, "More are converted in colleges, in proportion to the number of unconverted when they enter, than in any community or State. Eighty-eight ministers, who are pre-eminent in the Church as pastors, professors and presidents of colleges, from John Robinson, the leader of the Pilgrim Fathers in 1592, down to Edwards, Dwight and Alexander, were converted in colleges."

Pastors may look upon learning, in connection with faith, in hope or in fear, but they can not safely be negligent of it. Schools of learning are bound to exist, and if Christian men do not establish and control them, and keep them consecrated to Christian purposes, irreligious men will found them and control them in the interest of infidelity. The educational power of a country is the dominant power, and Christians should wield it for good government, industry, morals and Christianity. If this is to be done, pastors must share in the work, yea, lead in the work.

Pastors, in their direct work in saving souls and leading them to a higher life in Christ, find peculiar aid in promoting *the* evangelical spirit. That spirit is a great need in schools of learning. When it is wanting, they become scholastic and corrupt. It depends greatly upon pastors to preserve that spirit. When in the dark ages they lost it, and became corrupt, the colleges and monasteries shared the same fate. Pure gospel in teachers and pastors will preserve pure learning. When Wickliffe, Luther, Calvin, and all the reformers, brought back a pure gospel, they revived and purified the systems of education.

Luther and Calvin saw that the Reformation could not be advanced without good schools. Luther established a system of public schools which lasted for a hundred years in Germany, and Bancroft says, "We boast of our common schools, but Calvin was the father of popular education, and the inventor of the system of free schools." Thanks to him, then, the Puritan pastors caught the spirit that secured a teacher for every fifty families, and a grammar school for every hundred. It was no doubt from his example in founding a college with eight professors, for the education of young men to preach the Gospel, that the New England pastors, only eight years after their landing, founded Harvard College. Those early pastors, Cotton, Hooker and Elliot were scholars of Oxford and Cambridge. The ten pastors who founded Yale College in 1700, partook of their spirit, and these men gave permanency and character to religion and learning in the Colonies.

It is impossible to estimate fully what power and influence pastors gave to education in the New England Colonies, and by it to Christianity.

But they furnish marked examples for pastors now, and in the future.

How can the pastor best perform his duty in education?

The apostolic injunction, "Let them learn first to show piety at home," serves as a *rule* for education in the family. Here the pastor's work should begin. I am now speaking of Bishops who are husbands and fathers. The exceptions are not worthy of notice.

The pastor should care for the education of his children, and superintend it with the vigilance of a good teacher; and so set an example in his own family which will inspire other families to seek education for their children. Thus he will become the means of elevating the standard of education in the Church and in the community. There are memorable examples of pastoral fidelity in home teaching. The father of Jonathan Edwards was a Hebrew and Greek scholar, and he took great pains to train his son to habits of study and analysis. The father of Dr. Ryland, an eminent Baptist clergyman of England, put into his son's hand a Hebrew grammar before he was five years old; and when yet but a child, he read to the pious James Hervey the twenty-third Psalm in Hebrew. In his visits, the pastor must not regard suggestions as to the best mode of directing the child's early education, as out of his sphere. Such guidance will aid in religious culture, will encourage parents in their toil and care for their children, and will stimulate the children in study.

In new portions of our country, the pastor can render great aid in establishing common schools, select schools and academies. He can exert an influence in securing good teachers, and if possible, Christian teachers.

Where schools are established, the pastor should visit them, speak in them, give honor to the teacher's calling. inspire the children with a love for study, and show them that perfect character is attained by a union of learning and religion. He should be willing to serve on boards of education and examining committees, to aid parents in choosing schools for their children, to direct them to those of their own denomination, and to prevent them, if possible, from sending their children to Catholic schools. Pastors should visit the colleges of their denomination, when they are near, in term time and at examinations. Such visits will remind the students that there is a vital relation between the colleges and the churches, between learning and religion, and will also cheer the professors in their work. A head officer in one of our leading Eastern colleges complains of a lack on the part of pastors in this duty. None come to see whether their work is well or ill done. He feels deserted by his brethren, and wishes our pastors would take lessons from other denominations. Pastors should also seek out and encourage young men to study for the ministry.

It is the duty of the pastor to remember our colleges and seminaries, and all schools of learning, in prayer, in his family, and in the pulpit. Such a remembrance renders institutions of learning in a manner sacred. In his sermons learning should be frequently commended as needful for all, and not simply for ministers, as though all the demand for educational force in the Church were confined to the pulpit. The churches need educated laymen and women. Such persons aid the pastor and the Sabbath-school; and learning thus consecrated to Christ gives character and enlarged influence to the Church.

Pastors are liable to fail in this. Says President Anderson : " I have heard sermons on the need of an educated ministry, but never heard a pastor in his own pulpit plead for an educated membership. Yet our churches are suffering for want of this. Our people have little idea of the need of an educated membership, beyond the standard of the common school." The pastor should have a care for teachers' meetings; prepare them for, and be present at them. By this means he will educate the whole Sabbath-school in the Scriptures.

He should recommend a religious paper. Luther Rice connected with foreign missions Columbian College and the "Columbian Star" as necessary means of their success. Does not this meeting, and do not these reporters of the press, confirm his views?

The pastor's care should be to organize and sustain educational societies, the precursors of our colleges, and seek for them a partial support in endowment. The American Education Society has a fund of seventy-three thousand dollars. The endowment of colleges and theological seminaries should be a part of his care. He would do well to remind his rich members of John Harvard, who bequeathed half his property and all his library to Harvard College; of Nicholas Brown, whose name will be perpetuated in Brown University; of Vassar, Shurtleff, Wm. Jewell and Samuel Payne; of Hamilton and John P. Crozer.

It is a part of the pastor's duty to explain to his people the dependence of our government upon the educated men of our colleges in framing constitutions and laws, in advancing the mechanical arts, in improving our common schools and academies. For these last the colleges furnish for the most part the teachers and the text books. But chiefly should he show the dependence of Christianity upon them for educated, pious laymen and ministers.

It is for the pastors to disabuse the minds of their people of the idea that colleges are merely secular institutions for the promotion of an educated aristocracy. In truth they are Christian schools, and were founded for Christianity. " *Pro Christo et Ecclesia*," the motto of Harvard, is in spirit that of all our colleges. The ten pastors who founded Yale are an example of the origin of our American institutions of learning.

The colleges of New England were born of the churches; and many of their pastors were born, both intellectually and spiritually, of the colleges. "Churches and colleges," says Professor Tyler, "sustain the relation to each other of alternate fountain and stream." If they are to continue in this efficient, refreshing relation pastors must bear an indispensable part in securing this beneficent result. Dr. Dwight once remarked to a pastor, that "the man who would show to common minds the connection between colleges and the interests of the Church would be a benefactor to his species." One competent to judge says: "We behold in Dr. Dwight the very demonstration which he asked. He corroborated revelation by the light of nature and reason, and at the same time brought it to the apprehension of the common mind. He transformed Yale from a nursery of infidelity into a Christian school."

It is for the pastor to maintain such a relation between colleges and churches that both shall unite in echoing the sentiment of Dr. Witherspoon, the scholar of Edinburgh, the President of Jersey College, the leading member of our first Congress — " Cursed be all that learning that is *contrary* to the cross of Christ; cursed be all that learning that is not *coincident* with the cross of Christ; cursed be all that learning that is not *subservient* to the cross of Christ."

It is the duty of the pastor to educate the church to observe the last Thursday in February as a day of fasting and prayer for colleges. Unless the pastor sees to this it will not be done. He has historical encouragement to do this. The converting Spirit has been granted from its first observance. In thirty-six different colleges fifteen hundred were converted in fifteen years. Revivals have averaged once in four years since the observance of that day.

As to the bearing of pastoral care in education, upon a general, effective, denominational *movement* in education, one church educated by its pastor to a correct view of the relation of colleges and churches, of learning and religion, would be a great power for good. The same result effected by ten thousand pastors in seventeen thousand Baptist churches, with a million and four hundred thousand members, would be a far mightier power; a rapid and general advancement would thus be made in our denominational character and influence.

Editors, professors, and presidents of colleges must do much in this movement; but it can not become general and efficient without the active co-operation of pastors in the work. The people are not self-moved to great reforms and upward progress. It is the work of educated men to enlist and lead them in such enterprise. By Tyndale's talent and learning the Christian people of his time were brought to read and love the Bible. Luther and Calvin taught their followers to cling to justification by faith. Roger Williams inspired his adherents with the love of soul-liberty, and with the resolution to retain and diffuse it.

Pastors, by their near connection and sympathy with the churches, and by their ability to see the true relation between churches and schools of learning, are peculiarly fitted to create a general and deep interest in education. In all the history of the Church, education has declined or prospered according to the corruption and ignorance, or to the purity and intelligence of the pastors. A pure, evangelical spirit in the teachers of schools and the pastors of the churches secures alike the interests of piety and learning. The revival of this gospel purity in pastors and teachers has ever been followed by the revival of pure learning in colleges, and by the establishment of public schools among the people.

Franke, of Germany, the pious pastor of Erfurt, the Dwight of Halle, the founder of the pietistic school, which numbered at one time five thousand students and one hundred teachers, is a representative of many pastors within the last five hundred years.

Professor Schmidt, in his "History of Education," says: "The lack of an evangelical spirit in the pastors, and their want of interest in the schools, retarded education in the last part of the eighteenth century." It was then that the godless sentiment of Rousseau obtained currency — "Let not the rising generation hear a word about God." It was then that some educators said — "Bring forth everything out of the idea, out of thyself, the world, the commonwealth, even the Deity."

It is the work of pastors to counteract this theory of education, and to maintain and exemplify the dependence of pure, practical education upon a pure gospel. It is their pre-eminent work in the sphere of education, to form such a union of life and sympathy between the churches and the schools as will infuse a Christian spirit into the latter and a Christian intelligence in the former. When all pastors and churches hold such a relation to schools, there will be a progressive and general movement in education, toward the perfect goal of thorough.learning, for the profit alike of science, of civilization, and of Christianity.

As to the bearing of pastoral care in education upon our denominational *character*, it is obvious to remark that the conditions of individual character apply to communities and nations, to churches and denominations of Christians. In the individual Christian, good talent, learning and piety constitute superior character. The greatest of the three is piety — the ground-work of all. Moses, Daniel and Paul, are marked characters of the *three* qualities combined. A denomination of Christians with average natural ability, united with learning and piety, will take character alongside the individual of like qualities. As *individual* piety is circumscribed in influence when associated with ignorance, so is it in churches and Christian bodies.

Christ is a prophet no less than a priest. Denominations obtain character through the talent and learning of their leaders. We can trace one to Calvin, another to Luther, one to Cranmer, another to John Cotton, and another to John Wesley. The names of Gill, Robert Hall, Carson, Fuller, Staughton, Broadus, Wayland, with living scholars whose names are quoted by pedo-Baptist writers as authorities in Bible translation and exegesis, give honor to the Baptist denomination in the sphere of learning. But where did those men of history, who have given name and honor to their denominations, with the exception of the Baptists of Waldensian antiquity, get their characteristic stamp? As Clement and Origen received theirs in the first Christian school of Alexandria, in the second century, so Jerome, Wickliffe, Erasmus, and Tyndale, obtained theirs at the universities of England and Germany, Luther at Erfurt, Calvin at Paris, Cotton, Cranmer and Wesley at Cambridge; Gill — being a heretic — was not admitted to the schools of the Established Church, but obtained his title from them by self-culture. Hall studied at Bristol and Aberdeen, by favor of Lord Coke; Roger Williams at Cambridge, Staughton at Bristol. History tells us that denominations receive their origin from the learning and piety of their *leaders*, and these leaders derive their *power* of intellect and learning from the *colleges*. Self-educated men, says a learned teacher, are half-educated; it is the college that gives fullness of character. In proportion as such men become numerous among the ministry of a denomination, will the entire denomination have character for intelligence and learning.

As to the bearing of pastoral care in education upon denominational progress, if there is any truth in the proverb, "Knowledge is power," it follows that education is a power for denominational progress. Without it, Congregationalists and Presbyterians would not stand among the first in influence. May we not trace their prosperity to the fact that they have founded the majority of colleges and theological seminaries in our country? Education does not necessarily result in a rapid increase of the numbers of a denomination, but education does give it permanent and pre-eminent character. According to Dr. Brooks' estimate, for fifty years previous to 1864, of five leading bodies of Christians, the Baptists stand second in numerical progress, the Methodists being first. It is true that neither have been *leaders* in education. But had they not become enlisted in education they would not have made so rapid progress, nor would they give such promise for the future.

The Baptists of America, from 1775 to 1855, increased from 380 churches to 14,070; from 350 ministers to 9,476; from 65,000 members to 1,322,469. Like our country, they have doubled in numbers every twenty years. It has been estimated that the same rate of increase in two hundred and thirty-six years, would find every adult member of our race, old enough for church membership, in the Baptist denomination, even if the population of the globe should be multiplied four-fold.

This progress in the past fifty years can not be separated from a new and progressive movement in the cause of education. It has been an indispensable aid.

The translation of the Scriptures into thirty-three languages, and the preaching of the gospel in all these tongues, have been effected by fifteen men of our denomination, educated in twenty-two colleges and five theological seminaries. Of our foreign missionaries, nine were educated at Rochester, thirty-seven at Newton, and forty-seven at Hamilton. These men, with an equal number of educated women, have sent forth 203,382,898 pages of printed truth, 79,356.784 pages of Scripture, and led thirty-five thousand heathen souls to Christ. (See Dr. Smith's Jubilee Report)

In regard to the rapid progress of our denomination in our own country, let us keep in mind that seventy-five years ago we had only Brown University, but now fifteen colleges; then no theological seminary, now six of high character, besides six schools for the colored people; but few educated men, yet within the last fifty years more than three thousand graduates from the colleges of the North alone have entered the Baptist ministry.

With our present position in education, and for the first time in the history of Christianity, with a free field, neither trammeled by the civil government nor persecuted by other Christian sects — Baptists have a mission vast and glorious. May they have faith, knowledge and spirit to seize upon the opportunity for civilization and education for Christ and His Gospel.

We, as pastors, have noble examples before us in the Puritan pastors of New England; in their successors, who are following the star of empire, and have already established schools west of Iowa, and on the Pacific coast; and to be more specific, in Dr. Elliot, the apostle of Unitarianism in the West, who has lived in St Louis thirty years, and founded Washington University, with an endowment of eight hundred thousand dollars, and whose name will be perpetually associated with the destiny of that grand city by the Elliot Public School for girls.

We are also inspired to duty by the venerable Baptist fathers, Stillman, Bowles, Manning, Sharp, Furman and Staughton.

We find the true key to success in evangelization in the example of Luther Rice, in whose mind missions, a college, and a periodical were kindred and inseparable interests. Hence he established Columbian College and the "Columbian Star." Baptist pastors have done much for education in their families and in founding schools. Forty-two of their sons have graduated at Rochester during her twenty years' history. The schools of Iowa and Missouri have been established by them. The same is true in other States. Some of them are bright examples in this city, one of whom has gone over the sea to recruit his exhausted energies, and writes me, "I have given a thousand dollars, and my church has given forty thousand, for the cause of education at Chicago, and I know the burden of these interests on the brain and heart are exhausting."

The forces which formed an era in our progress fifty years ago, must be relied upon for the future. First, an evangelical spirit, then educational societies, colleges and theological seminaries.

We must not over-estimate the power of education in converting men. An uneducated man in Northern Missouri, known as Uncle Jimmie Lillard,

6

has baptized over two thousand during his ministry. He is more an exhor-
ter than a preacher. Yet it is none the less true that education in the ministry and in the people gives power in the world, and steadfastness and perfection in religious character. Says Neander, when speaking of the ignorance of preachers and people in the second century, while admitting that
the Gospel was faithfully preached and sincerely embraced : "Christianity
will not long maintain itself in purity unless it enters deeply into the intellectual development of the people." This thought should be placed beside
one uttered by his pupil, D'Aubigne : "Alas for the land of Leibnitz and
Humboldt; a few Baptist preachers, having an experimental knowledge of
the sin of man and the grace of God, are far mightier for good to that
empire than all her Olshausens, Hengstenbergs and Strausses."

Pastors, above all men, have a mission in perpetuating a union of learning and religion, which, leavened by an evangelical spirit of progress, will
conquer the world for Christ. In this union we may look with bright hopes
for the future character, progress and usefulness of the Baptist denomination.

The paper was referred to the Committee on Denominational
Work in Education.

The report of the Committee on Scientific Education was then
read by the Chairman, Prof. E. OLNEY, of Michigan, and adopted.

REPORT OF COMMITTEE ON SCIENTIFIC EDUCATION.

The Committee to whom was referred the subject of "The Place of Scientific Studies in Present Education," and the paper on this topic by President
Talbot, of Denison University, would enumerate the following propositions,
as what they consider to be the opinions of our wisest and safest educators,
and as the sentiments of the able and judicious paper submitted to us :

First. It is desirable that a more thorough and extended course in scientific studies be secured in our regular classical college course.

Second. It is not desirable that the present courses in Latin, Greek,
Mathematics, or Philosophy be abridged either in extent or thoroughness.

Third. In order to these ends, it is desirable and practicable to steadily
increase the requisitions for admission to the Freshman class. Especially is
this practicable in the pure mathematics, the elements of the natural sciences, and perhaps in the rudiments of the French and German languages.

Fourth. That for young men generally, what is usually known as the
regular classical course is best, both for purposes of full and symmetrical
development, and as the basis for special or professional training and for
practical life.

Fifth. That, in institutions whose resources will permit, it is eminently
wise to establish different *courses*, such as the classical course, the scientific
course, the engineering course, etc., in order to meet the wants of specialists,
made such either from choice or necessity. But an indiscriminate eclecticism
is a serious evil.

Sixth. That the granting of the same degree for these different courses,
and especially any attempt to make the degree of *Bachelor of Arts* mean anything less or different from what it has hitherto represented, is to be deprecated as unwise and unjust.

Respectfully submitted,   EDW. OLNEY, *Chairman,*
                            AMOS N CURRIER,
                            O. HOWES,
                            J. E. JOHNSON,
                                    Committee.

The report of the Committee on the Increase of the Ministry and Theological Education, was read by the Chairman, Rev. N. M WOOD, D.D., of Illinois, as follows:

REPORT OF THE COMMITTEE ON THE INCREASE OF THE MINISTRY AND THEOLOGICAL EDUCATION.

The papers referred to this Committee on the subjects, "How Christian institutions of higher learning, academies, colleges, universities and theological seminaries, keeping progress with the growth of society, can best be built up in the West, with due regard always to other necessary expenditures of money for religious purposes," and "The duties of Western Churches with reference to the perpetuation, increase and education of the ministry," were listened to by the Committee, in common with the Convention, with exceeding interest; and though they do not feel called upon to give an indiscriminate indorsement of every sentiment therein expressed, they do feel a great satisfaction in commending these papers to the thoughtful attention of all our brethren in the Churches. We do not desire to occupy time or space by the further discussion of these topics in this report. In respect to the increase of the ministry and the facilities for theological education, your Committee have no new theories or plans to propose, and believe that they will have done all that may be expected of them when they urge the duty of the Churches to pray the Lord of the Harvest that He may send forth more laborers into His harvest, and give expression to their thorough conviction of the wisdom of that policy which avoids the diffusion of strength in multiplying schools, but rather concentrates and intensifies effort upon the establishment and endowment of a few first-class literary and theological institutions, centrally located, where such as are called to the ministry may be suitably trained for the work.

N. M. Wood,
E. Nesbit,
S. Tucker,
D. P. Smith,
F. A. Douglas,
Committee.

The report was adopted.

The Committe on Denominational Work in Education then reported, through the Chairman, President G. W. NORTHRUP, D.D., of Illinois, as follows:

REPORT OF COMMITTEE ON DENOMINATIONAL WORK IN EDUCATION.

The Committee to whom was referred the subject of Denominational Work in Education, beg leave to report —

That the subject is one whose claims upon the earnest and prayerful attention of the denomination, are enforced by the weightiest considerations. If we consider the relation of education to Christian civilization, and to the growth and power of our denomination; if we consider, also, the large number for whose intellectual and moral and religious training we are specially responsible, and the manifold agencies to be employed in awakening among the people a deeper and wider interest in education, and in guiding the

interest thus awakened to the best results, we are impressed with the magnitude and difficulty of the educational work with which the providence of God
has intrusted us. As means of accomplishing this work, we would particularly suggest the frequent presentation of the claims of education to churches
by pastors; the public advocacy of the same cause by educators of large experience and recognized ability; greater use of the press in influencing public
opinion upon educational questions, and united and vigorous organized
efforts, under the leadership of men of comprehensive views and practical
wisdom.

The Committee would submit the following resolutions for adoption by
the Convention:

(1) *Resolved*, That we recognize, with gratitude to God, the indications
of a more general and profound conviction of the importance of Denominational Work in Education, as seen in the desire of our churches to be
informed on this subject in all its aspects and relations; in the public advocacy, by educators themselves, of the claims of high culture; in the more
adequate endowment of our higher institutions of learning, and in the
organized efforts made to influence the public mind aright in relation to this
whole subject.

(2) *Resolved*, That, impressed with the conviction that the National Educational Convention, held in Brooklyn, gave an impulse to the work of
Denominational Education, the influence of which has been felt in every part
of the country, and also that a permanent National Organization is *essential*
to the highest efficiency of the efforts made to advance the cause which we
here represent, we would request the American Baptist Educational Commission to call another National Convention, to be held at such time and
place as may be determined upon by the Executive Committee.

(3) *Resolved*, That the interests of our Denominational Work in Education demand the existence of a Periodical, through which may be brought
before the people all important facts pertaining to the cause of education in
the several States, and the views of the most experienced and ablest educators as to the means of securing the highest prosperity of our various institutions of learning, Academies, Colleges, and Theological Seminaries; and
this Convention recommend to the Commission to take suitable means for
commencing the issue of such a Periodical at the earliest practicable day.

G. W. NORTHRUP,
For the Committee.

Dr. NORTHRUP said that during the past five years a great
progress had been made in the cause of education among the Baptists of this country. And much of this is due to the labors of the
Educational Commission, of which Dr. Cutting is Secretary. He
advocated the necessity and desirableness of an educational periodical. He said that what was needed was correct information brought
before the minds of the people; and he wished to take this opportunity to enter his protest against certain views which had been
advanced by several on the floor of the Convention, to the effect that
people of the West could only be interested in education by false
representations respecting the nature of our institutions. He
thought it was a libel upon the intelligence of our churches to say
that they must have presented to them something that " sounds

large." He believed that it was only necessary to present the truth, and present the claims of higher education upon its own merits.

Dr. CUTTING made some remarks on the adoption of this report, and in exposition of the objects of the Educational Commission, and upon the general subjects which had come under discussion during the sessions of this Convention. He said that he supposed the National Convention, to which allusion had been made, would be held — probably in Philadelphia.

The report of the Committee was then adopted.

Prof. SHEPARDSON, of Ohio, from the Committee to which had been referred the paper of Dr. Wayland on the Education of Women, read a report as follows:

REPORT OF THE COMMITTEE ON THE EDUCATION OF WOMEN.

The Committee to which was referred the paper read by Dr. Wayland, of Franklin College, upon Woman's Education, beg leave to report:

That we regard this subject as one of vast importance in carrying forward the great work of evangelizing our race, and hail with profound gratitude the interest it is now everywhere creating. Not only in the United States, but in various nations of Europe, and even in Asia, the subject is discussed, and schools for women established. There are already about fifty thousand females in the schools of Hindostan. Wherever Christianity goes, it creates the thirst and necessity for higher culture in woman as well as in man.

In our own country, the influence of Mrs. Emma Willard, Mary Lyon and kindred spirits, begins to be widely felt. Vassar's princely gift marks an era. Two individuals in Massachusetts, a man and a woman, have recently left to this cause, in the aggregate, one million and eight hundred thousand dollars. Others will follow such examples. The conviction is becoming deep and general, that the God-appointed teacher of our race should herself be educated. The world can not afford longer to lose the power of her higher culture. The millions are pre-eminently under her influence. As mother and teacher, she molds their characters in the impressible, forming period

In literature, too, as well as in the family and the school-room, she is making her influence felt. She has recently borne off several of the highest premiums of our liberal publishers. She is receiving in this department, in a few instances, three and four thousand dollars per annum.

Equal advantages are generally conceded to her in the public schools and academies. If she has produced no great work in science or in philosophy, so far as she has had opportunities she has demonstrated her abilities. In our best city schools she has borne off her full share of public honors. May she not now advance to a higher culture? Does not society need her cultivated talents?

Your Committee rejoice in the great work that has been performed by many of our female seminaries, and earnestly recommend that they be greatly strengthened by more ample endowments. It is unjust, not to say cruel, to continue to give by millions for the education of our sons, and so little for that of our daughters. In some way, equal provisions should be made for them.

The question of joint education of both sexes in college is not one of talents, morals or manners. There are constitutional differences that may not be ignored, in determining the precise conditions under which the highest culture shall be received, though the intellectual and moral nature of each is essentially the same. We see no way in which woman can receive a truly liberal education in less time or at less expense than man. There may be great room for an honest difference of opinion whether it is best to subject them to the same curriculum. There may be feminine graces and accomplishments, special aptitudes and necessities, that require for her, in her different sphere, to some extent an elective course. This question will be settled by mature thought and more extended observation and experience. The demand of the age is, that she be no longer neglected and deprived of the force, breadth and earnestness of Christian character which the most liberal culture can bestow. The great work now before us seems to be, to create and foster more just, enlightened and Christian views on the main question. In this way we can call out a vast amount of talent and means to elevate the social mass and evangelize the world.

D. SHEPARDSON,
For the Committee.

The report was adopted.

After a brief address by Secretary CUTTING, the Convention adjourned with prayer by Rev. GEO. W. HARRIS, of Michigan.

MARK H. DUNNELL,
President.

E. C. MITCHELL,
Secretary.

SUMMARY OF ATTENDANCE.

	VISITORS.		DELEGATES.	VISITORS.
New Hampshire	2	Ohio	11	8
Vermont	2	Michigan	18	6
Massachusetts	6	Indiana	8	12
Rhode Island	1	Illinois	18	58
Connecticut	4	Missouri	4	3
New York	13	Iowa	13	17
New Jersey	4	Wisconsin	8	14
Pennsylvania	2	Minnesota	5	3
South Carolina	2	Nebraska		1
Louisiana	1	Canada		3

Delegates.. 85
Visitors 162
Total attendance,... 247

NOTE.

AMERICAN BAPTIST EDUCATIONAL COMMISSION.

It is proper to subjoin to these Proceedings some account of the Educational Commission, in whose operations the Western Baptist Educational Convention had its origin, and to put this Convention into its proper historical connections.

The Baptist Educational Commission was formed November 20 and 26, 1867, and commenced its operations January 1, 1868. It was formed upon two distinct yet related conceptions. First, that the desires and efforts of a limited number of persons in the direction of the establishment, endowment, and working of our institutions of higher learning, were not met by a corresponding popular interest in education,— such an interest as was required to fill them with students, and to make them the blessings to our families, to our churches, and to society, which they were intended to be. Second, that the increase of our ministry, not in respect to numbers alone, but in respect to aggregate intellectual force and furnishing, was below the provisions made and attempted for such increase in our theological seminaries, and below the demands arising from the condition and increase of our churches, and the condition and tendencies of our civilization. It was hence an organization to promote both " Education and the Increase of the Ministry." It was a very simple organization. It was made up of a few gentlemen who united to sustain, at their own expense, an appeal for an advance in popular interest in higher education, and an appeal for a ministry replenished and augmented according to the necessities of the times in which we live. It proposed to stir the popular mind and heart, to spread enlightenment in respect to the value and importance of higher education itself, stimulating the interest therein of parents and of pastors, and to awaken and sustain in our churches a more prayerful and earnest attention to the great question of their future ministry. If it should be successful; if new thoughts and purposes in respect to education should so seize and hold our public mind generally, creating a new tendency and drift; if so the question of the ministry should rise to its true character as the first question of the instrumentalities by which the gospel is to be spread and its triumphs won,— then, indeed, would our institutions be filled, and be made in character and strength equal to every growing necessity, and then would the day of reward come for the cost of founding and maintaining them. It was, in a word, an attempt to promote education from the popular side, as an outgrowth of popular interests and demands, and to promote the increase of the ministry from the prayers of an enlightened and practical faith pervading the mass of the members of our churches.

The immediate occasion of the organization was the remarkable

interest in these objects which was awakened in the New York
Baptist State Convention, held at Poughkeepsie in the autumn of
1867, when a committee was appointed to whom the effecting of
such an organization was referred. This Commission, so formed,
had for its sphere of operations the States of New York and New
Jersey, but it was neither intended nor possible to restrict its inqui-
ries, its labors, or its influence within prescribed boundaries. It
contemplated, indeed, in its constitution a possible enlargement to
the breadth of the denomination. It proceeded to its work by col-
lecting facts, by appeals through the press, and by the addresses and
correspondence of its Secretary. It proved to have struck a chord
which vibrated widely. It started at once a new order of discussions
in the press of the denomination, and the information which it gathered up and published from every quarter, primarily for effects within
its own sphere, produced similar effects in remoter States. The
facts elicited and the questions discussed were of common interest,
and became the more an inspiration and a force by the magnitude
of the area over which the community of interest existed.

This common interest, so widely awakened, led to the calling of
the National Baptist Educational Convention which met in Brooklyn in April, 1870. At this Convention delegates from academies,
colleges, theological seminaries and education societies in nineteen
States and the District of Columbia, were assembled, continuing
their sessions through three days, and discussing and taking action
upon a great variety of topics relating to education. By this Convention the Baptist Educational Commission was requested to prefix
the word "American" to its name, and to spread its work over the
whole country. It was desired among other things to call local
conventions of similar character, and ultimately to summon another
National Convention. In pursuance of these recommendations the
Commission proceeded to enlarge the sphere of its operations, and
to call local conventions. The first assembled at Worcester, Mass.,
for New England, May 3d and 4th, 1871. The second was the
Western Baptist Educational Convention whose proceedings are
here given. Both these Conventions were largely attended, and their
proceedings indicated an encouraging growth, alike in the compre-
hensiveness of the views of education prevailing in the denomination, and in the vigor and success with which the cause of education
is advanced. Another Convention is to be held for the South, at
Richmond, Va., July 4–6, in the present year, and another still is
earnestly invited on the Pacific slope. Besides all these, a Southern
Convention, born of the National Convention at Brooklyn, and mod-
eled after it, a Convention numerously attended and influential, has
been held during the present year in Alabama. These are all signs
of a living and advancing interest in education which can not perish
without enduring fruits.

INDEX.